ADVANCE PRAISE

"Raw, real, and inspiring, Chad Dunn's story is proof that transformation isn't about perfection—it's about relentless ownership, disciplined action, and the courage to rewrite your identity. This book is more than motivation; it's a blueprint for anyone serious about changing their life."

—Ryan Bernardi
Head Coach, Prolific Prep, America's Top Basketball Academy

"Chad masterfully weaves a complex, gritty, and inspiring life story with honest lessons and actionable steps to self-transformation. A true joy to read. Perfect for anyone seeking to better themselves and gain control of their future."

—Anthony Quintana
Owner, Infinite Imagination Productions LLC

"*Mind Over Virtually Everything: 10 Codes to Transform Your Life* is exactly what the title says. No matter what stage of life you're in, there's something in this book that'll shift your perspective. Chad makes you think differently about yourself, your habits, and what's possible. The life you want is at your fingertips and this book might be the push you need to go get it."

—Madison Conner
Professional Basketball Player

"If ever there was a question as to whether good people make bad choices—over and over again—this book has an answer for you. Chad Dunn is a prime example that self-evolution is real, and that life is truly what you make of it."

—E. Davis
Probation Officer

"Chad Dunn writes with rare vulnerability and humility, making the lessons feel both relatable and deeply impactful. He shares hard-earned wisdom with honesty and heart. The codes he lays out are not only practical—they're transformational. A must-read for anyone serious about personal and professional growth."

—Mary Ellen Androsky
Founder, Professor, Fractional CMO, Board Member Novah Media

"MOVE is a must-read story about overcoming the challenges of life with purpose and the right mindset. It's motivating and empowering, showing that ANYONE has the capability to build a foundation for a better tomorrow. This cautionary tale of growth and redemption literally takes you from the trap house to the boardroom, filled with belief, perseverance, and love. Chad's journey will truly MOVE you!"

—Curtis Brown Jr, MBA
Entrepreneur-Program Director, ABC Skills, LLC.

"This book blends raw personal storytelling with ten life codes aimed at empowering readers to transform their lives through intentional decision-making, mindset mastery, and personal accountability. This is a must read for all CEOs, business leaders, parents, and anyone looking to take accountability in all aspects of their life."

—Jordan Spurgeon
Sports Journalist, Sports360AZ

"Chad Dunn's incredible journey from federal prison to successful CEO is nothing short of extraordinary. His 'Mind Over Virtually Everything' philosophy isn't just inspiring theory; it's a battle-tested roadmap packed with practical wisdom and a game-changing, nine-step plan that can transform any life, no matter how broken or hopeless it may seem. I'm blown away by Chad's authenticity, his tenacity of spirit, and his proof that with the right mindset and unwavering commitment, second chances can become the greatest chapters of our lives."

—Lori Schumaker
Speaker, AACC Certified Christian Life and Mental Health Coach,
Author of *Surrendered Hearts*, Founder of Unveiling Hope at LoriSchumaker.com

"This is a must-read for everyone. No matter who you are—where you come from, what you believe, or what role you play in the world—this book offers something essential. If you're someone who wants to understand how things work and, more importantly, how to change them, this book is the tool that will help get you there. It's insightful, powerful, and deeply relevant. Don't just read it—absorb it, use it, and let it guide you forward."

—Rachael Lea Blackwell
Track Operator, Chandler BMX

"The ability to realize that the correct mental attitude allows you to overcome the greatest obstacles in life and the key to every successful warrior. Chad's book shows you how changing your perspective can take your lowest of lows in life and turn them into a positive strength and motivator. Phenomenal job showing the only thing that can stop you is you."

—Travis Rowland
U.S Army Paratrooper, Career Police Officer

MIND OVER VIRTUALLY EVERYTHING®

MIND OVER VIRTUALLY EVERYTHING

10 CODES TO TRANSFORM YOUR LIFE

CHAD DUNN

Mind Over Virtually Everything®: 10 Codes to Transform Your Life

First Published in the USA in 2025 by Peacock Proud Press, Phoenix, Arizona

ISBN 978-1-957232-29-4 Hardback
ISBN 978-1-957232-30-0 Paperback
ISBN 978-1-957232-31-7 eBook

Library of Congress Control Number: 2025917090

Editors
Laura L. Bush, PhD, peacockproud.com
James Thole
Chelsey Drysdale

Cover and Interior Design
Medlar Publishing Solutions Pvt Ltd., India

Headshot Photo Credit
Kaine Vieira

For my Grandson River,

Life won't define you; you will define yourself through the choices you make and the values you live by. Follow the codes with intention, and you will win your game.

Everything in life starts with one in a row. One right choice. One disciplined action. One quiet victory no one else sees. Stack them. Repeat them. That's how strong lives are built— brick by brick, moment by moment.

You are the creator of your identity. Build with wisdom. Move with a purpose.

With all my love in you,

Grandpa

TABLE OF CONTENTS

INTRODUCTION:
NINE WEEKS IN HELL

OCTOBER 20, 2003

It's 7:00 a.m. on a Tuesday morning as I step out of my parents' bathroom, fresh and clean. I've always been particular about staying clean—I hate feeling dirty. Walking into my room toward my dresser, something moving catches my eye outside the open window. Still feeling nervous about last night's deal, I walk closer to get a better view. The scene unfolding in front of my parents' house changes my life forever: a caravan of police vehicles from every jurisdiction blocking our cul-de-sac, two heavily armored SWAT vehicles parked at the front.

Vehicle doors fly open, and eight to ten officers carrying shields and guns sprint toward our house. I hear my mother's bedroom door open.

"Here they come!" I yell.

"Who's coming?" she asks.

"The SWAT team!"

I sprint past her to the front door, wearing just boxers, pulling my shirt over my head as I run. I don't want them destroying my parents' home. I need to open the door before they break it down. They're about to kick it in by the time I get there.

"We have a search warrant. We're coming in!"

"I'm opening the door!"

I save the door just in time and yank it open. Before I can speak, I'm thrown onto the entrance floor and cuffed, as people flood into my parents' home. The hard floor pushes into my cheekbone. From the corner of my eye, I see Chandler police officers, Phoenix police officers, undercover officers, and DEA agents flooding into the house. When my mom appears, I shout, "She has nothing to do with this. Don't hurt her!" I feel the cold barrel of a SWAT member's rifle press against my temple, pinning my head back down. Then I see my English bulldog, Lucy, run outside and an officer raise his weapon.

"Don't shoot her!" I scream. "She's friendly!"

They don't shoot, and Lucy sniffs around the yard, enjoying unexpected freedom before they tell my mom to put her away so they can release their search dogs. They lift me to my feet and sit me at the formal dining room table. I'm thinking my intuition about last night's drug drop was right. I knew those two unmarked cars in the motel parking lot looked suspicious. I should have left the scene. Now they're tearing through my parents' house, and I can see my backpack sitting on the couch where I left it last night. Inside that bag are five hundred ccs of testosterone, hundreds of Percocet pills, and a half pound of marijuana. If they open that up, I'm really screwed.

"You have an arrest warrant out of Hawaii. Tell me what you know," an officer says. "You're looking at twenty-five years to life."

Hawaii? Shit, this has nothing to do with last night. This isn't something my mother needs to hear. "I don't know anything," I tell them. That ends the interrogation. They take me outside to a waiting police cruiser. In the back seat, I find my codefendants, Roman and Mario. We sit there for about an hour while law enforcement and dogs continue to search my parents' house.

We all know why we're there, but nobody says anything. We bullshit and try to keep the mood light, not knowing what's coming next. Finally, the vehicle starts to move. It takes us to a holding facility for processing. The first thing I notice is the smell—body odor mixed with disinfectant and a cocktail of other offending odors I can't identify. Thirty-six prisoners packed into a single holding cell; violent offenders mixed with nonviolent ones. Many are fresh off the streets, unwashed and wild-eyed. The air is frigid. The cold seeps into my bones.

They know about Hawaii, but how much they know, I don't know. The next day, they take us to see a judge, and he reads our informal charges—informal because the judge in Hawaii will formally charge us since that's where they're saying the crime was committed. Mario gets offered bail with his parents' house as collateral. Roman and I don't make bail. That's when it hits me—this is different from any trouble I've been in before.

After four nights of constant noise—shouting, fighting, doors slamming—they wake us before dawn. "Line up for transport!" The chains clank with every movement as they load us onto a stripped-down Greyhound bus.

The bus heads toward Phoenix Sky Harbor but turns off before the main terminals. We pull up to a restricted gate where a plane sits surrounded by U.S. Marshals. The morning sun glints off their badges as they wait to escort us aboard. My first *Con Air* flight.

The plane lands 951 miles later at the Federal Transfer Center in Oklahoma City—the same facility Timothy McVeigh and the

Unabomber once passed through. The plane taxis directly to the jail terminal, so our feet never touch the ground. We shuffle down the jet bridge, chains still clanking, to meet another group of detention officers.

"If you want a HOT and a COT tonight," an officer announces, "I recommend donating your clothes for processing. The choice is yours." I want that cot and hot food. The decision is easy. I donate my clothes.

For eight days, I share a cell with an old Confederate guy from South Carolina. We pass time playing Scrabble, the plastic pieces clicking against the board. One game on the first day he plays "WATCHADU."

I challenge it. "That's not a word."

He grins and drawls, "Yeah, it is. What'd you do?"

Right then I know I'm a long way from home.

After eight days of uncertainty and no contact from my family, I'm put on another flight. This time it lands in Los Angeles. Riverside County Jail is my new home for the next two weeks.

The jail layout is two-tiered—state inmates on the bottom tier, federal on top. Walking up the stairs is like running the gauntlet. State inmates line the bars, catcalling: "What's up, homie? What you in for? How much time you looking at?"

A white inmate by the stairs tosses me an ounce of tobacco and a lighter.

"Take this up there with you man. You'll be good."

I pocket it quickly and keep moving. The federal tier holds about forty inmates, mostly South-Siders. When I try to claim the only remaining bunk in the Homie section, they're on me right away.

"You ain't one of us. Your section is over there."

I look to where they point, but I don't see any available bunks. I know I need a place to sleep, so I try to connect with them and make a peace offering. I speak some Spanish, make conversation, and share the tobacco. Suddenly I'm accepted. First lesson in prison economics: Having something others want provides you with protection.

After two more weeks, they process me out again and load me into an eight-passenger van. We drive onto the LAX tarmac and pull up to a United commercial flight bound for Honolulu. Four of us inmates, each with our own marshal, board first through run-way stairs before the jet bridge connects. They put us in the very back. Regular passengers file on later, some trying not to stare at the marshals' uniforms. I keep my cuffed hands still in my lap, try-ing to blend in despite my prison clothes.

Four hours later, through the plane window, I catch my first glimpse of Hawaii—not how I remembered seeing it the last time I was here. After landing, they drive us in a van to the Federal Detention Center. More processing, more strip searches. "Face the wall, lift up your ball sack, turn around, bend over, grab your ankles and cough."

They put me in another room for medical screening. Three questions: Any diseases? Vaccinations? Tuberculosis shots? Already got those in Oklahoma. Then the last question.

"Have you ever thought about committing suicide?"

"No," I say.

But when they ask Roman the same thing, he jokes, "Yeah, I'm thinking about it right now." Bad move. They strap him to a chair and put him in a straitjacket heading for the padded room.

They take me upstairs to a unit with cells arranged around the perimeter of a large dayroom. Two people to a cell. My cellmate is Fa'Fiti Fuamatu-Ma'afala, cousin of Chris Fuamatu-Ma'afala, the former Pittsburgh Steelers running back. He's a big Samoan guy, in for a probation violation—failed drug test. He claims it was from performing oral sex on his girlfriend who was using drugs. I have to laugh. I've heard every excuse in the book, but that's a new one. I like him more than my last cellmates already.

The unit dynamics are complex. Just like everywhere else in prison, there are racial divisions, but here it's different. Instead of just Black and white people, you have Hawaiians, Tongans, Samoans—and they don't all get along. Being the "haole boy" from the mainland, I have to be careful. But having made runs to Hawaii before, I understand enough about their culture to stay respectful.

They feed us well, especially at Thanksgiving. While other facilities serve mystery meat and powdered eggs, here we get huge turkey legs, fried fish, and Kahlúa pork. The guards know better than to short-change these massive Polynesian inmates on food. They will riot if they're not fed well. Plus, many of them have family working as corrections officers, which keeps things relatively peaceful.

Through my window, I can see the ocean and watch planes taking off all day. It's a strange kind of torture being so close to paradise but locked away from it. At least I have a view, and the conditions are better than the holding facilities I'd been kept in up to this point. I spend my time reading, playing cards, and watching the planes.

Finally, nine weeks after I was arrested at my parents' house, after my grandmother posts $25,000 bail, I walk out of the Federal Detention Center. The bright Hawaiian sun hits my face—the first time I've felt it directly in nine weeks. I'd traded my street clothes for a cot and a hot meal back in Oklahoma, so my only options are to grab some clothing from the donation box. The only things that fit me are a Hawaiian-style button-up shirt and some Z. Cavaricci jeans. I look like a clown, but I'm a free clown. My pro bono attorney, Dwight Lum, gives me $100 for travel, and because they'd taken all my possessions, including my ID, my parents ship my old ID to Dwight's office. After finishing with Dwight, I take the public bus to the airport.

I've been stripped, searched, shackled, and shipped across the country multiple times. I've learned the complex social hierarchies of different detention facilities, navigated racial politics, and survived the system's grinding processes. But I've made it. I don't know what's coming next. I'm just happy to be going home.

TWENTY YEARS LATER

I stand in the middle of MOVE® Human Performance Center watching a professional athlete train alongside someone learning to walk again after a spinal cord injury. The 5,455-square-foot facility hums with purpose—physical therapists guiding rehabilitations, trainers working with elite athletes, people from all walks of life pushing their limits and redefining what's possible.

This isn't just a gym or physical therapy clinic. It's a testament to the power of transformation. The same drive that once led me down destructive paths now fuels my mission to help others overcome their own challenges. Whether I'm working with an NBA prospect chasing their dreams or someone fighting back from catastrophic injury, the core truth remains the same: Your past mistakes don't determine your future success.

I know this firsthand. That morning when SWAT teams surrounded my parents' house could have been the end of my story. Instead, it became the beginning of a new one. The federal prison system did what it was designed to do—it broke me down. But in that breaking, I found the seeds of rebuilding. I discovered that the same intensity that had made me successful in the drug game could be redirected toward positive goals. The hustle that had put me behind bars could be transformed into legitimate entrepreneurship.

But transformation isn't just about changing what you do. It's about changing who you are. In prison, I learned that character is all you have when everything else is stripped away. Today I apply that lesson in every aspect of my business and life.

This book isn't just my story. It's a blueprint for anyone who wants to rewrite theirs. Through my journey from convicted felon to CEO, I've identified ten fundamental codes that govern personal transformation. These aren't just theories or motivational slogans. They're battle-tested principles that I've used to rebuild my life and that I now use to help others build theirs.

Whether you're an athlete recovering from injury, someone struggling with addiction, or a business owner fighting to survive, these codes will show you how to harness your experiences—even the painful ones—and transform them into fuel for future success. You'll learn how to create a new identity built on character rather than credentials, how to turn adversity into advantage, and how to become the author of your own story instead of a character in someone else's.

The truth is everyone has something they need to overcome. Everyone has a past they need to transform into a better future. At MOVE, we see it every day: the high school athlete battling back from career-threatening injury; the executive struggling with chronic pain; the burn victim learning to grip again. Different challenges, same fundamental truth: On the other side of pain lies greatness.

This is what I want to share with you—not just my story, but the principles that made my transformation possible. The same mindset that helped me survive federal prison now helps MOVE clients push through their own barriers.

You might be thinking, "But you don't know my situation. You don't know what I'm dealing with." You're right. I don't. But I do know this: Whatever you're facing, whatever mistakes you've made, whatever obstacles stand in your way, you have the power to transform them into stepping stones toward something greater. I've seen transformations happen too many times in prison, in my business, in the countless lives we've touched at MOVE to believe otherwise.

This book is your guide to that transformation. Through these pages, I'll show you how to apply the ten codes of Mind Over Virtually Everything® to your own life. You'll learn how to break free from negative cycles, build unshakable self-belief, and become the person you were meant to be. You'll discover that when you learn to control your reactions to your thoughts, you unlock the power to transform your life.

The journey won't be easy. Transformation never is. But if there's one thing I've learned, it's this: Your greatest challenges contain the seeds of your greatest opportunities. You just need to know how to cultivate them.

Are you ready to begin?

Let's move!

CHAPTER 1

BECOME WHO YOU ARE

"Knowing yourself is the beginning of all wisdom."
—Aristotle

If you ever visit the Temple of Apollo at Delphi, you'll find the inscription "Know thyself." The phrase is often attributed to the ancient Greek philosopher Socrates. Various Greek writers, including Plato and Aristotle, mention it in their works. The phrase is a cornerstone of Greek philosophy and emphasizes the importance of self-awareness and understanding one's own nature, limits, and potential.

The ancient Greeks are credited with creating the philosophy that built Western civilization, and I believe their focus on the self and identity was their greatest gift to us. Everything in life, good and bad, starts with your self-identity. This is the biggest lesson I've learned after fifty-plus years on this planet.

When you start digging around and doing research on identity, you find volumes of complex definitions and entire books on the topic. It's easy to get lost in what you uncover. But the more you look, it becomes clear there's no universal definition, even among all the "smart people."

I think it's most useful to keep things simple when you can, so I've chosen the three most impactful components that create self-identity. I've found that when you understand how your DNA, beliefs, and actions influence your identity, you have the foundations you need to create a version of you that you love.

MY DNA

My DNA is linked to a man named LaFayette Dunn. He was my great-great-grandfather. At age thirteen, he mounted his horse and set out to make his claim in life. He left his family behind in Owensboro, Kentucky, and headed west in search of something better. He made his way through Oklahoma, Kansas, and into the San Juan Mountains of Colorado, where he prospected for gold—unsuccessfully.

After time in Utah, he came back to Silverton, Colorado, and worked in the mines. One day, traveling from Silverton to Durango, he came across two German sisters in a buggy. He ended up marrying one of them, Johanna, and together they settled in Durango, Colorado, and homesteaded a 180-acre ranch, which remains there today on Pleasant View Mesa.

Three generations later, my dad, Scott Dunn, was born at that ranch. His dad, Bill, ran cattle at the ranch, which had expanded to more than five hundred head of cattle and ten thousand acres of grazing territory since LaFayette hammered the first stake into the mesa. Ranch life for my dad meant tending to the animals every day, including weekends and holidays. It meant starting work with the sunrise and stopping with the sunset. Ranch life is hard, and it forms hard people.

My dad left the ranch after he graduated from high school, but the ranch never left him. I saw the homestead toughness in my dad as a child, and I admired it. He'd often skip breakfast and lunch because there was work to be done. He ran a construction business—another way to make a living through hard work—but he was forged for it through his upbringing. Hard work was in his DNA and became a defining characteristic of his self-identity.

My mother, Judy, met my dad in Durango, after her family moved there for business when she was eighteen. Mom's family history gave her business DNA. Dad was an athlete and met Mom while running sprints. I guess he must have run fast enough to impress her because they were married in 1970 after two years of dating. My sister Holly was born in Durango in 1971. Then the family moved north to Fort Collins, where I showed up in 1974.

Why am I giving you this background information about my family?

To become who you are, you need to understand the beginning ingredients that came together to shape you in your formative years. The ingredients that shaped me are adventure, hard work, and an active lifestyle. You can't choose your DNA, but you can understand it and choose which parts are worth embracing and which parts you need to adjust as you grow.

THE FIRST VERSIONS OF ME

My parents bought me a BMX bike when I was six years old. It was a standard Schwinn BMX model, nothing fancy, but it might as well have been made of gold the way it made me feel. The moment my hands gripped those handlebars, everything changed.

"There's a BMX track in Fort Collins," Dad said one morning. "They have races. Want to check it out this weekend?"

Of course I wanted to check it out. I'd been riding that bike nearly nonstop during sunlight hours since the day I got it. Racing around with friends in the neighborhood was what I lived for, and now I was being told I could do it on a stage with people watching. Life couldn't get better than that.

The track looked massive through my six-year-old eyes—a twisted maze of dirt hills and banked turns that made my stomach flip. Bikes and riders were everywhere, their numbers on their plates saying it all—number one was the top-rated rider—new riders got to choose a number over forty. The other riders' gear was far more professional than my regular clothes and basic bike. I clutched Mom's hand as we approached the registration table.

"First time?" the woman asked, smiling down at me.

I nodded, suddenly unable to speak. She handed me a paper plate to place on my handlebars with the number forty-seven on it. Standing at the starting gate for my first race, I gripped my handlebars so tight my knuckles turned white. Seven other kids lined up beside me, some in proper racing jerseys, others wearing plain cotton long-sleeve shirts like me. Everything was quiet. Then the mechanical click-click-click of the starting gate dropping pierced my ears.

Everything happened at once. The gate dropped. Pedals spun. Dirt flew. Wind rushed past my ears. The first jump sent my stomach into my throat, but I held on. Banking into the first turn, I found myself in third place. By the second turn, I'd moved into second. The final stretch felt like I was flying. My mind felt empty. I was racing in the moment.

Still in second place, I crossed the finish line, my heart pounding so hard I could barely hear the cheers. Mom and Dad were at the finish line, both grinning ear to ear. But it wasn't their smiles that hooked me—it was the feeling. The speed, the jumps, the competition, the achievement. In those few minutes on the track, I'd discovered something about myself.

That night, still buzzing from the race, I asked Dad if we could go back next weekend. He smiled, probably remembering his own childhood dreams of riding horses like his grandfather LaFayette.

"Every weekend if you want, buddy."

I didn't know it then, but that simple "yes" would shape the next decade of my life. BMX racing wasn't just a hobby. It became my first real identity. Those early races taught me something crucial about becoming who you are: Sometimes you have to take a leap, even when it scares you. Sometimes the most terrifying jumps lead to the best landings.

My parents became my biggest fans and made my development possible. Mom drove me to practices and all the events. The more someone raced, the more points they gained, and their ranking increased. They also got more reps in and became a better rider. A year into racing, I'd reached "expert level" and was racing across Colorado state lines into Laramie, Wyoming.

The more I rode, the more I won. I started outfitting my bike with better components. I upgraded my riding gear from a long-sleeve off-the-rack plain cotton shirt and jeans with a pant leg strap to an official racing uniform. I was now wearing co-factory gear from GT Bicycles. My new uniform came with yellow racing pants, or "leathers" as we called them. The pants were made of nylon for protection and had a matching jersey to fit. Front and center on my chest was the big GT logo with wings coming off the letters. When I put that uniform on, I felt like I could fly. My identity as a BMX racer was solidifying. I was no longer a weekend racer. I had become a legitimate competitor on the circuit.

Two years into my BMX racing career, I'd climbed my way to the eighth-ranked racer in the state of Colorado. My beliefs and actions had manifested my identity into something I took pride in. Then everything changed. The recession hit in 1982, and my dad lost his construction business. My parents made the difficult decision to leave Colorado and move to Arizona. Everything unfolded in a matter of weeks. When we arrived in Arizona, we didn't have a permanent residence, so we stayed at a KOA campground for three months until my dad found work and earned enough to get us into a home.

As difficult as I'm sure that was for my parents, I don't remember feeling like anything too bad had happened. Despite the hardships, my parents continued to support my racing. By this time, my sister Holly had started racing too, and she was winning even more than me. My parents knew it was important for us to stay busy, to keep moving, to stay active, so they stepped up when they had all the excuses in the world not to. While my dad was working hard to rebuild his family and get a job, my mom was hustling to take care of us kids every day. She was shuttling us all over town for practices and races, keeping us fed, and continued to be our biggest cheerleader.

Despite being uprooted from the place I grew up and leaving all my friends behind, the thing that hit me the hardest after I moved to Arizona was not a sense of loss or living in a campground—it was losing. The Arizona guys were good. The level of competition had increased substantially because kids in Arizona can ride year-round. I went from top ten in the state in Colorado to the middle of the pack in Arizona. I soon realized I was now in a different game, and if I was going to stand a chance at winning and holding onto my identity as a top BMX racer, I'd have to put more work in.

My sister and I stepped up our games and put in the work. It led us to full-ride sponsorships from a local bike shop called Bike Barn. That meant better bikes, nicer gear, and everything paid for. We kept grinding and started racing at the national level, which meant Mom and Dad were now driving us across state lines again. As soon as I made my way to the top of the Arizona riders, I found out the California racers were even better. I kept working hard, and I made my way to the number-one rider in my age group in the state of Arizona, and top three in the nation at age fifteen. Holly had risen to number one in the nation! We'd reached the pinnacle of success in the BMX world at the time.

My racing days are some of the best memories of my youth. We traveled the country with incredible families and made friendships I still have to this day. But nothing lasts forever, and at age fifteen, at the top of my game, I was at a crossroads. My identity had been BMX racer for a decade. Doing one thing for ten years at a high level will teach you a lot about that thing and, more importantly, yourself. I knew if I wanted to continue to keep winning, I'd need to put even more work in. It was only going to get more difficult. I was now a freshman in high school, and a whole new world of opportunities started to open up. The new thing that was stealing my attention away from racing was football.

Dad played football at Colorado State. At one point, he went head-to-head with the NFL Hall of Famer Mean Joe Greene. I'd always looked up to my dad, and if I could play football like him, at a high level, I felt that would be something worth pursuing. I didn't have the passion and commitment for BMX racing I once had, so I made the choice to step out of that identity and start a new one. I was going to be a football player. I knew I had football DNA and was athletic enough to compete at a high level, as I'd proved with my BMX career. What I didn't realize at age fifteen was that success in one area of life doesn't translate to all areas.

If you know anything about football, you know size and strength are an advantage. You wouldn't know it looking at me today, but when I was a freshman in high school, I was barely five feet tall and weighed 125 pounds. My high school had two freshman football teams: the normal one and the peewee squad for smaller kids. I played on the peewee squad. I had a good freshman campaign and held on to hope that I'd hit my growth spurt between freshman and sophomore year. If I got more sleep and ate more, I was sure I'd start looking like a Dunn man.

By the time sophomore year came, I hadn't grown an inch. The weight scale hadn't moved. I knew if I joined the football team, the only playing time I'd get would be at practice. I had a choice to make. I knew enough about myself to know I wouldn't be happy riding the bench, so I chose not to play football.

The identity I held for nearly a decade as an elite BMX racer had ended. My new identity was supposed to be as a football player, but that was no longer an option. I didn't know what to do. I felt defeated. I wasn't going to be the football player my dad was. My dad, however, didn't care about that. He saw that I was down and made a suggestion.

"Why don't you try wrestling?"

"Wrestling?" I asked. "There's no way I'm going to roll around with another guy in tights and sweat all over each other."

Dad laughed, then gave me some perspective.

"Wrestling is hand-to-hand combat. One-on-one. Mano a mano. It's the only way you can beat up another guy and not get in trouble."

Hearing it put that way got my attention. Like BMX racing, wrestling isn't really a team sport. You can win a championship on your own, even if your whole team falls short. Size and strength don't matter as much because wrestling has weight classes. This clicked with my personality, and my dad was suggesting it, so I knew it would make him proud. My new identity became a wrestler.

The great thing about wrestling is the discipline it teaches you. Make weight or you don't compete. Making weight requires a healthy lifestyle. When other kids started drinking in high school,

I didn't take part. When you're wrestling, your body is a temple, and everything you put into it is under a microscope. Although I wasn't aware of it at the time, wrestling was keeping me out of trouble.

Your identity changes over the course of your life, especially when you're young and trying new things. Trying on one new identity can lead to a new one you might have never encountered otherwise. The greatest gift wrestling gave me was an injury. At the start of my senior year, I separated my shoulder and tore my labrum. It resulted in me missing the most important year of my wrestling career, but it also opened the door to my future. That injury led me to a physical therapy room, an entire new world I didn't know about. These professionals helped people every day. They worked with athletes. They were changing people's lives and doing meaningful work.

I was in my last year of high school, and I knew the next big step in life was coming. Being in that therapy room with those physical therapists and seeing what they did, I thought I could see myself doing that and enjoying it. I remember thinking, *That's who I want to be. I can see myself doing this.*

Little did I know, the detours I would take and the identities I would go through before becoming that version of myself.

WHY SELF-IDENTITY MATTERS

Carl Jung, the famous Swiss psychiatrist, once said, "The privilege of a lifetime is to become who you truly are." Remember, the first code to becoming you is understanding and acknowledging the power you have over creating your self-identity. When you start thinking about how your mind influences your actions, you discover that you have a view of who you are and act it out. To learn how to control and shape it, you must first understand why self-identity matters.

Self-identity is the foundation upon which every aspect of your life is built. It's the lens through which you view yourself, make decisions, and interact with the world. It's deeply personal. It shapes how you view your place in the world and your relationship with others. It's not just a passive reflection of who you are, but an active force that influences your thoughts, behaviors, and life choices.

When you have a strong, clear sense of self, you're better equipped to navigate life's challenges and pursue your goals with confidence. On the flip side, a weak or undefined self-identity leads to confusion, insecurity, and a sense of being lost or unfulfilled.

When you're a child, you form a sense of who you are based on feedback from the people around you and your interpretations of success and failure. My early identity was elite BMX racer. I got continual feedback from the people in my life that this was accurate, and the results of my actions told me this was true. I was fortunate to have such a positive experience around my identity during my early years. Not every child is born into a positive environment. Over time, these influences slowly solidify, and your identity grows stronger, but this does not mean it's fixed. It's solid, but it's not granite. I didn't remain an "elite BMX racer." My identity kept transforming.

The best way to take control of your identity is through self-reflection. Examine your thoughts, beliefs, and behaviors. Ask yourself questions like: *Who am I? What do I value? What are my strengths and weaknesses?* This process helps you become more aware of the aspects of your identity that may have been formed or influenced by external factors. The more you understand about who you are now, the easier it becomes to identify areas in your life that you want to change. Write down your thoughts so you can see how your self-awareness develops over time. You can't change what you don't see, and the more time you spend in that headspace, the stronger you'll get at using it to your advantage.

LEARN TO IGNORE THE NOISE

Taking control of your identity isn't a layup. Many external and internal forces can make your journey difficult, including societal pressures and past mistakes. These factors will control your self-identity if you let them. They are the voices you hear outside and inside your head that tell you lies and encourage you to give up. You must learn to ignore them to become who are you.

Society often dictates norms and expectations about who we should be based on factors like gender, age, race, physical stature, and socioeconomic status. These pressures can influence you to act in ways that do not reflect your authentic self. For instance, societal expectations might push you into a particular career path or lifestyle, even if it doesn't align with your passions or values. Over time, these external influences can shape your self-view in ways that feel disconnected from who you are.

Your experiences, particularly negative ones, also play a significant role in shaping how you see yourself. Traumatic events, failures, or abusive relationships leave lasting imprints. These experiences can lead you to create a false story about yourself that holds you back from unlocking your true potential. When left unchecked, the voices gain strength, and your past self keeps you from transforming into who you can be.

Ignoring the noise is difficult, but there are tools you can use to weaken its power. Start by building resilience. Resilience is the ability to bounce back from adversity and continue moving forward when things don't go your way. For instance, when you lose a game, a game perhaps that you did not play well in, you have two options: (1) Submit to the voices in your head that tell you you're a loser. (You may even hear external voices saying the same thing); (2) practice resilience and acknowledge that you did not play your best, accept it, and ask yourself what you need to do to be better next time.

Did you finish all your reps in your workout or leave two on the table? Did you run the last sprint all out or give it 80 percent? Did you study for the full hour or close the book after thirty minutes? Building resilience isn't about getting down on yourself when you come up short; it's about being honest with yourself.

UNLOCK YOUR FULL POTENTIAL

Much of my life, I transformed through different identities, guided largely through my DNA and environment. But even with my parents trying their best to point me in the right direction, my external environment started to pull me into places that weren't good in my teen years, and because I wasn't thinking about who I wanted to be, the negatives began to overtake the positives.

When you don't think about who you want to be, you leave yourself open to ending up in bad places. Some people end up in good places regardless; many do not. Why risk it? I never told myself I wanted to be a drug dealer. I created stories in my head that told me I would be okay no matter what, and that was enough. To no surprise, none of those stories I told myself ended with me behind bars serving a three-year sentence in a federal penitentiary.

Prison has a way of getting you to think about who you are. It wasn't until I started to consciously think about who I wanted to be and what kind of life I wanted to live that I started to become who I am today. The beauty is you can start thinking about who you want to be right now. You don't have to stay where you are now. You're in control, you're the author of your future, and understanding that is the first step to turn your life into everything you want it to be.

THE FIRST CODE TO MIND OVER VIRTUALLY EVERYTHING:

You are in control of creating your self-identity.

MOVE Sound Bite Summary

1. Self-identity starts with understanding your foundations—your DNA, early experiences, and the environments that shaped you.

2. Your identity evolves through deliberate choices and actions, not just circumstance or inheritance.

3. Each phase of life brings opportunities to redefine who you are—identity is a journey, not a destination.

4. Building self-awareness through reflection and challenging limiting beliefs is key to taking control of your identity.

5. You must learn to ignore external and internal voices that hold you back from becoming who you truly are.

CHAPTER 2

YES OR NO

*"A real decision is measured by the fact
that you've taken a new action. If there's
no action, you haven't truly decided."*
—Anthony Robbins

When you're strapping stacks of bundled cash to your thighs in a Hawaiian hotel bathroom, you don't think about consequences. You're focused on the mechanics—making sure the rubber bands are tight enough to hold the bundles in place, but not so tight they cut off circulation. You're checking that the compression shorts hide any telling bulges, that your baggy board shorts look natural. Your mind is consumed with the immediate: Don't sweat, don't fidget, walk normally.

The money felt heavy against my legs as I made my way through Honolulu International Airport. Each step that I took I made a conscious effort to appear casual. I'd practiced this walk in my hotel room—not too fast, not too slow. The faces of officers blurred as I passed through security, my heartbeat steady but loud in my ears. I'd been assured this was routine, just a quick trip to paradise and back. Easy money.

Everything went perfectly. I played my part exactly as rehearsed—just another tourist heading home after a few days in Hawaii. No one looked twice at the white guy in board shorts and a long-sleeve Hurley T-shirt. When I landed in Phoenix, I felt invincible. I'd pulled it off without a hitch. The nervous energy that had powered me through security transformed into pure confidence. This wasn't just about the money anymore; it was about being smart enough, bold enough, to do what others couldn't.

That feeling of invincibility lasted exactly three months. When the U.S. Marshals knocked on my parent's door at 7:00 a.m. on that Tuesday morning, I realized too late that success had been the most dangerous part of that Hawaiian operation. It had made me believe I was in control, that I was choosing my path. Standing in handcuffs in my parent's living room, watching federal agents tear through their home, a question entered my mind: *How did I get here?* The answer was simpler than I realized at the time.

It happened one choice at a time.

THE POWER OF CONSCIOUS CHOICE

Many of the choices you make happen at the conscious level, while others work on an unconscious level. Because you can't escape choices in life, you make choices whether or not you think about them. The key to creating the life you want is to make all your important choices at a conscious level.

When you make conscious choices, you still make wrong choices, but over time, you can build your choice-making muscles and learn how to make better ones. A conscious choice is made with full awareness and deliberate thought—you're fully engaged in the decision-making process. You consider possible outcomes, weigh the pros and cons, and align the choice with your goals and values. Your mind makes multiple connections and works through a complex web of variables when you make a conscious choice. A conscious choice has a clear intention because you're aware of why you're making the choice and what you hope to achieve.

Conscious choices give you a sense of control over your life. They should involve reflection, analysis, and often consultation with people you trust. If you're struggling with a choice, that means it's important. Take your time with big choices and ask yourself questions like, *What are all the possible outcomes of this choice?* or *How does this choice align with my long-term goals?* Do an honest cost-benefit analysis; think about how the worst-case outcome would affect you and the people you care about most. If you make a conscious choice, and it doesn't work out in your favor, don't let it damage your identity; view it as an opportunity for growth.

When you make unconscious choices, that's when bad things can happen more than you'd like. Making an unconscious choice means you didn't spend enough time thinking about all the variables. Instead, you chose based on an automatic response out of habit, ingrained behaviors, or subconscious beliefs. Often you're not even aware you've made a choice until after the fact; that's where the feeling of helplessness comes from when you get stuck in the cycle of making bad choices. You feel out of control— because you are.

Part of my journey becoming who I am today involved a lot of reflection about the choices I'd made in the past, then taking ownership of those choices. If I were to blame my family, society, or some other external influence, I know my circumstances would never have changed. When things started falling apart for me, I wasn't weighing the consequences of my choices. I was living in the moment, not thinking about anyone but myself and what I needed to do to feel good right then. It felt amazing when it worked out, but the feeling was brief, and because I wasn't consciously thinking about who I was or what I wanted in life, I continued to make choices driven by immediate gratification. Worst of all, I wasn't happy, and I didn't even know it.

Once you've accepted that you're in control of who you become, you're faced with the challenge of creating that version of yourself. The act of consciously choosing is the tool you use to create your identity, but choice does not become choice until you act. Choice first begins in your mind as a thought, but until you act on it in the physical world, it has no energy or impact on your life. I know it might seem obvious when I put it this way, but how often do you tell yourself you're going to do something and never do it? You're not alone! Making conscious choices, then acting on those choices, is the key to becoming who you want to be.

THE BEGINNING OF POOR CHOICES

My pattern of rationalizing poor choices started long before that Hawaiian hotel room. My first step into this destructive pattern came during my freshman year at Arizona State University. The summer before classes started, I got caught up in the excitement of newfound freedom—like so many of my friends. One night, just before the first semester started, we planned a big party. Everyone was getting ready to move into the dorms, and the energy was electric. It was what you'd expect from a typical party thrown by soon-to-be college students—loud music, alcohol, and poor decisions.

I was never a heavy drinker, although I drank from time to time on the weekends. I always managed to stay out of trouble when I drank, but that night was different. At some point, a few buddies and I wanted to drive across town to another party near the infamous Manzanita dorm. I'd driven under the influence before, and nothing bad had happened, so I rationalized the pattern would continue. I'm positive I never thought twice about it before getting behind the wheel. On our way to the next party, we passed a cop, and my friend waved at him. Bad choice. The cop followed us and flashed his lights.

One buddy in the back seat was passed out, and my friend who waved at the cop was clearly intoxicated. I'd only had a few beers, but I was the one driving. We had a brief conversation with the officer, and I thought I was in the clear when he asked if I'd had anything to drink. I told the truth, and after a field sobriety test, I was arrested. My friend, the one who had waved, drove my car away from the scene with the officer's permission. In my mind, if my friend had never waved, I wouldn't have been arrested. Although that's probably true, instead of taking the incident as a warning from the universe, I interpreted it as bad luck.

Two years later, my high school buddy Omar and I had everything lined up for an unforgettable spring break week at Lake Havasu. MTV was going to be there, we had a houseboat rented, and about twenty friends were waiting for us. The last words out of my mom's mouth as we left the house were, "Don't drink and drive." Of course not.

We adhered to her advice until we were about thirty miles outside of Havasu and decided to start celebrating early. We both cracked open a beer, and I turned up the music. I had the car set on cruise control at ninety miles per hour with the sunroof open. We were barreling down Interstate 10 when we hit a massive wind shear. The next thing I knew, the car was sliding across the freeway.

I had no control. I overcorrected, and the car tire clipped the edge of the asphalt and dirt. We flipped about six times before coming to a stop upside down in a hayfield.

By some miracle, we walked away from that wreck. We even had the presence of mind to hide the beer cans in the bushes before highway patrol arrived. We'd survived a potentially fatal accident, and instead of seeing it as a warning, I interpreted our survival as proof of my invincibility. Even when a single forgotten beer can fell from the wreckage and led to my second DUI, I still didn't get it. More bad luck, I reasoned.

By the time I got my third DUI in Scottsdale a year later, I had perfected the art of deflecting responsibility. The night was winding down, and I needed to get home because I had to work the next morning. Again, like the first two times, I'd barely had anything to drink. And I still had the mindset that it was more bad luck than bad choices that had resulted in the arrests. It was around one-thirty in the morning, and when you're out at that time, it doesn't take much to get pulled over. I was going forty-three miles per hour in a forty-mile-per-hour zone when I saw the red and blue flash behind me.

This was my third DUI within a five-year time frame, so the Arizona DMV suspended my license for six months. After the suspension ended, I had to use a breathalyzer blower device every time I wanted to start my car. The consequences this time included thirty days in Sheriff Joe Arpaio's notorious Tent City, an outdoor jail in the scorching Arizona desert where inmates wore pink clothing and endured extreme heat. Even this didn't shake my conviction that I was just unlucky, not making poor choices.

What I couldn't see then was how each incident reinforced a dangerous mindset: that consequences were things that happened to me, not results of choices I made. This pattern of thinking—blaming circumstances, bad luck, or other people—would follow me into decisions far more serious than drinking and driving. I was building a foundation of self-deception that would eventually support the weight of much bigger lies, ones that would ultimately lead me to that hotel room in Hawaii, strapping thousands of dollars to my legs.

THE STORIES WE TELL OURSELVES

It's easier to create stories in your mind, and tell yourself you got unlucky, than take responsibility for your choices and make a change. While the DUIs were negative moments, overall I felt like my life was headed in the right direction, partly because it was true. I'd been working at a place called Q Sports Club as a fitness instructor and certified spinning instructor. I was doing the work I'd been studying to do and even had my own company: C It Dunn Health Improvements. In my self-deluded mind, I was ahead of schedule. In fact, I thought I was doing so well that I decided to stop taking my exercise science classes at ASU. I was already doing the thing. Without school in the way, I could make more money working, build my therapy skills with hands-on experience, and have more time for nightlife entertainment. I had my cake and was eating it too!

The new position was a dream job for a young guy like me trying to work his way into the sports medicine world. I loved being around collegiate, professional athletes, and the who's who of the Valley. I soon discovered that when you help people feel better—when you solve difficult problems that are impacting their lives in big ways—they are extremely grateful. So grateful that they become your friends and invite you into their worlds. Soon my circles of celebrity "friends" grew, and I entered the social life of athletes who get paid millions of dollars. This brought me a new level of nightlife entertainment that was intoxicating to the young version of myself.

Now I operated in two different worlds: one in South Phoenix, where I had connections from high school who were still partying in the rougher part of town, and one in wealthy Scottsdale, a scene filled with glitz, glam, and good taste. After spending more time socializing in Scottsdale, I discovered there was a high demand for certain "party enhancers" that I could easily acquire in South Phoenix for half the price. Always the salesman, I seized the opportunity to increase my cash flow. Another byproduct of being the guy everyone comes to for party candy was power and status. All of a sudden I became a lot more popular with the girls, so other high-status males wanted to hang around me. More money and higher status? That seemed like an easy choice to make.

I ran this operation by having Darren, a friend's brother from high school, go into the hood and buy what I needed. He was a junkie, so I'd give him some of whatever he bought. Then I'd take the rest and sell it. It was solely a business enterprise for me. I never tried the product—in the beginning. Then, a few months into this new "enterprise," Darren asked me to drive him into the projects on 24th Street and Broadway to pick up some shit because his car wasn't running. I'd never seen where he went. I always gave him the money to score, and I was curious, so I agreed to drive him. After making our way deep inside this unexplored territory, I knew I was in a place I'd never been before.

The contrast was stark. Windows were covered with bars and blacked out. Diapers and wheelless bikes decorated the curbs. When we entered the stash house, the smell hit me hard—a rank combination of garbage, dirty diapers, and other offensive odors I wasn't familiar with. A young Mexican woman holding a baby led us into the living room where the "cook" was waiting. When he saw me, he didn't look pleased.

"You a cop?" he asked.

Wanting to ease the tension, I greeted him in Spanish. Right away the mood in the room changed. I was speaking his language. My minor at ASU was Spanish; I was putting my education to work. Once I started speaking Spanish, it was as if Darren no longer existed. All the attention was on me. Speaking their language gave me instant credibility.

From that day on I continued making pickups with Darren, which helped me slowly build trust with the dealer. Eventually I cut Darren out and started operating on my own. I enjoyed the rush of going into this dangerous environment by myself, the only white guy for blocks. No other gringo from Scottsdale had the balls to do it; it gave me an adrenaline high. Over time, I met more dealers. They got to know me, and my reputation grew. Business was booming.

For about eight months, I followed the cardinal rule of drug dealing: Don't get high on your own supply. The cocaine never interested me because my nose had issues after breaking it when I wrestled, but smoking crack didn't involve snorting anything up my defective nose. One night I made a crack delivery to some "customers" after the clubs closed down for the night in Paradise Valley. They offered me a hit. It wasn't the first time I'd been offered, but for some reason, in that moment, I thought, *Let me see what this is all about.* I didn't fear becoming an addict. I was confident about my self-control. This was an experiment.

A guy loaded the crack into a small rose glass pipe. I lit the flame on the lighter, hovered it over the rock, and slowly inhaled—instant euphoria! The rush flooded through my entire body. My heart raced as a wave of warmth and energy surged through my limbs. Everything around me seemed to fade. The world shrank into a distant blur, leaving only an overwhelming sense of focused joy.

But as quickly as it came, the high began to slip away. It felt good. I could see why people liked it, but I didn't need another hit. I still felt confident drugs would never become a problem for me. I had too much drive and ambition. Then I started getting high on crack several times a week. In the beginning, the drug never slowed me down. If anything, it gave me a boost of productive energy. I was disciplined at first, only using when I was partying a few days a week. But the company I was keeping normalized crack use. I felt I could stop anytime I wanted. Why not enjoy myself? I was still a productive citizen making more money than I could spend. I taught my spin classes, trained my clients, and even found time for crack-fueled football games on the weekend. I was going full tilt and loving every minute.

Six months later, what had been a few days a week habit became a daily habit. Drug use began to negatively affect my work. For the first time in my life, I started missing workdays. Despite all the evidence in front of me, I still felt in control. In reality, I was slowly being sucked into a dark vortex that I lived inside for two years. Although I always had some kind of work, it became sporadic. At the tail end, the money I made selling was just enough to pay rent and support my habit. My enterprise was no longer profitable. I even had to ask my parents for rent money a few times during this period. They didn't know why.

One night, near my lowest point, a knock on the door saved me. I was sitting in my living room with a few fellow crackheads. Drugs were spread out all over the coffee table; we were in the middle of a three-day bender. Unfamiliar knocks on your door when you have drugs scattered all over the place, and you're halfway out of your mind, are the things of nightmares. After hearing the knock, all three of us instinctively froze and listened. I picked up the remote and muted the TV. After a few moments of silence, a voice spoke through the other side of the door.

"I know you're in there. You need to come out now."

It was my dad.

I knew this was a serious confrontation, and he wasn't going to leave. I didn't respond. I collected all the pipes and crack on the table. Then I put them in the master bedroom out of sight. My drug-using friends sat frozen on the couch. They had no idea who was on the other side of the door. Knowing Dad wasn't going to leave, I spoke through the door.

"I don't want you seeing me like this," I told him, hoping that would be enough for him to leave.

"If you don't open this door, I'm calling the cops!"

Considering the amount of drugs we had on us, I calculated opening the door was my best option at that point. I'd take the humiliation of being seen at my worst over jail. As I unlatched the deadbolt on the door and opened it, I was surprised to not only see my dad standing there, but my mom as well. Nobody said anything; there was nothing to say. I stepped aside, and they entered. They surveyed the scene and had the place cleared out in a matter of minutes. Then they took me home. I didn't resist. I think some part of me, deep down, felt relief.

HOW TO JUDGE THE QUALITY OF YOUR CHOICES

When my parents rescued me and took me home, they told me I'd be doing rehab for ninety days—at their house. They took my car keys, my driver's license, and my wallet. My therapy program consisted of crafting with my mom. As children, my sister and I did a lot of crafts while traveling for BMX to stay busy. Craftwork is calming and rewarding. It keeps the mind and body occupied in a positive way. But now, in my late twenties, I was confined to my parents' home doing craftwork. This wasn't the place twenty-year-old Chad imagined he'd end up. But this was the reality I'd created for myself. Compared to what happens to most crack users, I was lucky. Part of me knew that.

I completed a perfect ninety days of rehab. I even created some awesome stained glass work, got my mind straight, and stuck to the program my parents designed. Part of me didn't want to hurt my parents, and I felt relieved to not be living the way I'd been living for the past two years. My parents had pulled me out of the vortex, and I needed the reset. But after ninety days, I was itching to get out of the house. I asked my mom if I could go to Circle K to buy a Mountain Dew. She agreed.

Buying a Mountain Dew wasn't my plan. I knew I could get to the Southside and back home fast enough not to raise any suspicion. I scored a dime bag within minutes, grabbed my Mountain Dew, and was back at the house in record time. After sipping on my Mountain Dew, I went to my room and got high. The crack hit energized me, so I went out to the kitchen and did some more craftwork. I still felt like I was in control, so the crack wasn't a big deal, as long as my parents didn't know. All I had to do was play the role they expected of me, and eventually I'd regain my freedom, which I did, and I played it well.

To get out of the house and do something productive, I got a job working construction. I was free to go out during the day, but I stayed at home in the evenings. The good thing about working construction is I couldn't be high and do that kind of work. I was also required to take a drug test, which mean I had to stop using. I also felt like I was starting to make my dad proud because he was a construction guy. Everything was moving in the right direction for about four months until the construction company told me I needed to go out and work a job in Oakland, California. For most people, this news would mean little more than relocating for a job opportunity. For me, it meant I'd be going to the home of the rock—the crack rock.

It didn't take long for me to find that Oakland crack rock. Without my parents around, I could smoke every day now without anyone looking over my shoulder. My California trip ended when a pipe burst on a job site and burned my hand. I went back home to Arizona to get treatment at the Arizona Burn Center. That was the end of my construction career.

After healing, I took a part-time job as a bouncer at Graham Central Station a few nights per week and got another job working for O Premium Waters. I figured selling water in the desert couldn't be too difficult, and it wasn't. I quickly worked my way to one of the top salesmen in the company. But as I found new success with my work, I slowly began to revert to old patterns. I started hanging around with my old crowd from high school and soon got introduced to a drug enterprise they had going with a group in Hawaii. The scale of the operation was much bigger than anything I'd been involved with before.

At first my involvement was minimal—entertaining the Hawaiian guys when they came to town for payments. But when they needed a new way to get larger quantities of product onto the island, I had the perfect solution through the watercooler business. The coolers came in two sizes: an eighty-pound model that included hot and cold water and a twenty-pound model that only had room temperature water. If you took the lighter cooler and put it in the heavy cooler box, you'd have sixty pounds of free weight. Problem solved.

As the operation grew, the Hawaiians started getting concerned about the number of times they were flying into Phoenix. They felt it could be drawing too much attention and wanted some of the Phoenix guys to go to Hawaii to pick up the payments.

My friend Roman, who started the business, stepped up at first and flew into Hawaii and brought the money back on his own. Eventually he needed more people to help, so he asked if I was interested. All I had to do was fly to Hawaii, pick up the money, then fly home. My fee for one day of work and a couple days of sun on the Hawaiian beaches would be more money than I'd ever made in one day.

This time I thought about the consequences. Roman had done it successfully without any problems and walked me through the process. It wasn't as dangerous as going into the hood to pick up drugs. The only danger would be if I got stopped and they found the money on me. If I acted the part, everything would go smoothly. The only thing that could stop me was bad luck. After sitting on the idea for a day or so, I agreed.

Looking back now, every choice I made was a step toward that hotel room in Hawaii. Each decision seemed logical at the time— from the excuses I made after each DUI, to making that first drug run into the projects, to taking that first hit of crack. I kept telling myself I was in control, that I could stop anytime, that I was different. But the truth was I wasn't evaluating the quality of my choices by their outcomes. I was reacting, rationalizing, and repeating the same patterns, expecting different results. Some say that's the definition of insanity.

CHOICES ARE ALWAYS ABOUT YOU

It's critical for you if you're reading this book to understand that you can't take responsibility for anyone's choices but your own. This message is especially important for parents. The fundamental job of a parent is to protect their children and give them what they need to be independent adults. Part of those expectations is that your child will not only survive but thrive and live a healthy, prosperous life. Parents come in all different flavors. Many parents put in extra work to teach their kids how to be productive and successful people. It's those parents who hurt the most when their child fails to thrive in society. Often they blame themselves—and sometimes the child unfairly blames the parents.

I never blamed my parents. I knew they loved me and did their best to teach me right from wrong. They gave me the freedom to make mistakes, which I believe is critical to becoming who you are. Most importantly, if I would have blamed them, the chances of me making better choices in the future would have been much less.

My own children have made choices that have affected their lives in negative ways. They knew what not to do because I've always been transparent about what led me to prison. But hearing my story and listening to my advice wasn't enough to keep them from stumbling and sometimes stumbling hard. Every individual in this life must take their own path. As parents, it's our job to keep our children healthy and guide them. We must also know that we're raising human beings who have free will and will ultimately make their own decisions, as they should. When you remove being responsible for yourself and the choices you make, you lose your power.

THE SECOND CODE TO MIND OVER VIRTUALLY EVERYTHING:

Master the power of choice to take control of your life.

MOVE Sound Bite Summary

1. Every choice creates your identity. Make them consciously.

2. True choices require action. Thoughts without follow-through are just wishes.

3. Take full ownership of your choices. Blaming others keeps you stuck.

4. Judge choices by their outcomes, not your intentions or rationalizations.

5. The more you make conscious choices and reflect on the outcomes, the better you become at making good choices.

CHAPTER 3

IF YOU SLEEP WITH DOGS, YOU'LL WAKE UP WITH FLEAS

"Show me your friends, and I'll show you your future."
—Dan Pena

On December 30, 2003, I returned home from my nine-week trip through the criminal justice system. Now my life was in limbo as I awaited my sentencing. I knew I couldn't go back to the street life. I was facing twenty-five years in prison, so they said, and didn't want to add onto it. My pretrial release terms required me to be gainfully employed, so I went back to the fellas at Rehab Plus and asked if I could work with them. Rehab Plus had become like a second family to me. Despite my circumstances, they knew I was trying to make better choices. I began working full-time as a physical therapist tech and personal trainer, along with helping out with other tasks around the facility.

Back in Hawaii, my pro bono attorney, Dwight Lum, was doing what he could to help fight my case. I didn't know how long it would be until my trial, but I wanted to get this part of my life over as quickly as possible. The key, for now, was to stay out of trouble. The speedy trial I was hoping for didn't come, but I did manage to keep my nose clean for nearly a year until the contaminants in my environment got the best of me again.

One night I joined friends at Kona Grill, where we slammed a shitload of sake bombs. As the hour grew late and work loomed the next morning, I excused myself and slid behind the wheel. Despite the alcohol coursing through me, I reached home without incident—rolling the dice and coming up lucky. I barely considered the risk of another DUI, even though I knew my blood alcohol level exceeded the legal limit. Operating on autopilot, I navigated the roads with what felt like flawless precision.

I merged onto the freeway the next morning, cutting across three lanes without signaling to reach the fast lane. A few seconds later, in my rearview mirror, red and blue lights flashed. An unmarked car pulled up behind me. The officer approached my window.

"Do you know why I pulled you over?"

"The lane change?" My mouth felt dry.

He leaned closer. "Have you been drinking?"

I almost laughed. It was 6:30 a.m.

"No sir, I'm on my way to work."

"Step out of the vehicle."

The early morning air felt cool as I followed his instructions for the field sobriety test. Walk heel-to-toe. Stand on one leg. Follow the pen with your eyes. I felt steady, in control. When he pulled out the breathalyzer, I didn't hesitate.

"Go ahead," I said. "I'm good."

The machine beeped. The officer's expression hardened. "Point zero two."

My stomach dropped. Below the legal limit, but in Arizona, any alcohol in your system could mean a DUI. The implications hit me like a punch to the gut. I was on federal pretrial release. This could send me straight to prison.

A DPS cruiser pulled up. The new officer gave me a ride home, making small talk I barely heard. "If it'd been me who pulled you over . . ." he said, but I tuned him out. The words that kept repeating in my head were "violation of pretrial release."

I hired another attorney that afternoon. When he called a week later to tell me he'd gotten it reduced to a speeding ticket, I felt the weight lift. It was as if the universe was trying to tell me something, but I couldn't hear it. I called it bad luck, again.

Sometimes the simplest examples help us understand the most complex problems in our lives. Imagine planting six sunflowers in wooden boxes around your backyard. You give them all the same quality soil, water, and fertilizer, yet after a few weeks, two aren't thriving. They're drooping and wilting while the others flourish. You monitor them daily, wondering if they're diseased or if you've had bad luck with those two. Then you notice something: The struggling sunflowers are positioned in a shaded area, only getting morning sun, while the healthy ones receive full sunlight all day. After moving them to a sunnier spot closer to their thriving counterparts, the struggling flowers begin to recover. You needed to change their environment.

Like sunflowers, your environment determines your well-being in nearly every area of life. The right environment helps you grow and reach your full potential. The wrong one keeps you stagnant— or worse. Although human problems are more complex than plant problems, the impact of environmental change is strikingly similar. The main difference is that for plants it's about their physical environment, while for humans it's about our social environment. Simply put, you become who you associate with.

LIVING IN LIMBO

Over the next six months, I managed to make the right choices. Because my case was complex, with dozens of people involved, I'd now been living with the weight of my fate in limbo for nearly one-and-a-half years. I wanted it to end so I could know my fate and get on with my life.

I was on a good-fucking-choice streak following the last DUI scare that ended when a friend invited me to his house to watch the historic Arturo Gatti vs. Floyd Mayweather Jr. fight. The drinks were flowing all night, and because it was the weekend, summer, and the biggest fight in a long time, I decided I'd enjoy myself and got smashed with my friends.

Around 2:30 a.m. I had to go home. There are holes in my memory about what happened after that, but I do remember at one point seeing sparks flying after I hit something I later found out was a concrete median. I'm sure, at impact, my system dumped a bunch of adrenaline into my body, which helped me focus on the road again, but it was too late. My truck was in bad shape. I limped to the nearest exit, pulled off into a neighborhood, and parked on a side street. Then I got out to examine the damage.

Metal grooves carved deep into the passenger side of my truck glinted in the streetlight. Each dent told the story of my collision with the median—a story that ended with my wheel barely clinging to the axle. Even if I could clear my head enough to attempt changing the tire, the mangled rim wasn't going anywhere.

The flash of red and blue lights painted the neighborhood. Gravel crunched under boots as an officer approached, his flashlight beam piercing my eyes and casting my shadow long against the pavement behind me. My heart hammered as I squinted into the light. This became my stage now, and I had one chance to nail my performance.

"Evening sir."

His voice cut through the darkness. "Care to explain what happened?"

The lie rolled off my tongue, smooth as silk. "Looks like it has a flat tire to me, officer."

"That you do." His flashlight beam traced the mangled metal. "What happened?"

Another lie, even smoother. "Friend of mine—he was driving home from the bar, hit something."

"And where's this friend now?"

"Took off running."

The beam dropped from my face as he asked for my ID. I fought the spins while watching his silhouette in the patrol car. When he returned, something in his stance had changed.

"Mr. Dunn." He let my name hang in the air. "Let's go over your story again. You said your friend was driving?"

"Yes sir, that's right."

His flashlight swept past me toward the darkness behind. "See that car back there?" The beam caught a distant windshield. "They've been following you for five miles. Watched you hit the sidewall on the freeway. Followed you off the exit. Saw you—and only you—get out of that truck."

The spotlight felt hotter now, my rehearsed story melting away beneath it. I had nothing left to say. All I could do was stand there, caught in a lie of my own making.

When I thought back to all the DUIs prior to this one, I felt in control. I'd told myself they were all just bad luck. But this one was different. I could have killed somebody, and I knew it. Up to this point, I'd been making good choices. I'd stopped using drugs,

I was working, I was being a productive citizen. But the drinking had sucked me back into the vortex. I let down a lot of people who had stood by me despite my past choices, and that hurt the most. I was in a dark place, a place I never wanted to return to. But first, I had to get out of the place. That was the last night I ever drank alcohol.

Despite my terrible mistake, the people I cared about most didn't give up on me. They all chipped in, shuttled me to work, and kept supporting me as best they could. Shortly after the DUI, I hired a high school friend as my attorney to help with the felony DUI case. Our goal was to get it delayed until my federal case sentencing. If I was sentenced for the DUI case before the federal case, I'd be going into the federal sentencing with a felony on my record, which would result in a longer prison sentence.

I stayed out of trouble for the next ten months. Finally, near the tail end of 2005, after two years of living in limbo, my federal case started moving forward in Hawaii. My attorney, Dwight Lum, contacted me and told me people had started talking. They were taking plea agreements. He found out I was named as one of the money mules in the case. My official sentencing date was scheduled for May 31, 2006. I could finally move on from this chapter in my life.

Now that we knew the sentencing date for my federal case, my DUI attorney stopped requesting extensions and scheduled my sentencing for June 1, 2006—the day after my federal case sentencing. Everything was going as planned. I never imagined I'd feel so relieved to go to a sentencing and face twenty-five years in prison.

MY SENTENCING

On May 31, 2006, I flew to Hawaii with my dad for my federal sentencing. The court went through all the procedures for thirty minutes. I delivered a handwritten letter to the judge and gave a short speech acknowledging my mistakes, showing remorse and promising to be a better citizen in the future. When I finished, the judge delivered my sentence.

"Mr. Dunn, we did have a chance of a probation sentence in this case due to your minor role in the operation. However, I must take into consideration the actions you chose on your pretrial release. You were not supposed to drink alcohol. Yet you chose to. Not only that, but you chose to drive while under the influence, putting both yourself and others in serious danger. Due to your consistent poor choices, I feel it's in your best interest to feel the consequences of your actions in a more severe way than probation. I sentence you to thirty months in federal prison."

It felt like time stopped. The room went silent. Nobody moved. After what seemed like minutes, but was only a few seconds, the judge picked up his gavel and slammed his desk. Wham! A sharp crack echoed through the room. It sent a jolt through my body.

The judge's voice broke my trance as he granted my request to self-surrender within forty-eight hours in Arizona, allowing me to stay near my family during my sentence. I had made that plea in my presentencing report. Had authorities detained me in Hawaii, I might have landed in a federal facility anywhere in the US. Though my lawyer had cautioned me about a potential two-year sentence for violating my pretrial release, the two-and-a-half-year term still left me reeling. It beat the twenty-five years prosecutors initially warned me about, but three years behind bars still isn't easy time.

After sentencing, the judge ordered me to a bail revocation hearing across the hall. Having violated probation with my DUI, I faced the risk of immediate custody, which would cost me my $25,000 bail and make me miss my DUI sentencing the next day.

When I faced the next judge, I didn't know what to do, so I did the best thing I could by taking full responsibility for my actions. I apologized for violating my pretrial release, admitted to my mistakes, and promised to never return to a courtroom. The judge must have sensed I was genuine, and the last judge had already sentenced me, so this judge granted my request. I got lucky.

That night I got on a red-eye with my dad out of Honolulu to make my third courtroom appearance in less than twenty-four hours back in Phoenix. The third judge sentenced me to eight months in state prison for the DUI the next morning. I expected that much. Initially I thought I was now looking at thirty-eight months behind bars, but the judge allowed me to serve the eight months concurrently with my federal time. Lucky again.

The next day, on June 2, 2006, my girlfriend Jackie drove me to the Sandra Day O'Connor federal court building in Downtown Phoenix to self-surrender.

A NEW ENVIRONMENT

The marshals handcuffed me and took me through some doors and back to an area of concrete holding cells. After nearly ten hours waiting, they escorted me and another group of self-surrender prisoners to a van and transferred us to the Corrections Corporation of America facility, the same place the feds took me after my first arrest nearly three years ago when this all started.

What most people don't realize is that the processing and holding centers are a much worse environment than the actual prison facility. When I arrived at the CCA holding center, thirty-six prisoners were packed into a single holding cell. Nothing separated deranged violent criminals from nonviolent ones like me. For many inmates coming in, the holding cells were their first stop post-arrest, which made sanitation a big problem. Many had been living on the streets or wandering through the desert for weeks before they entered the holding cell. Their bodies reeked, and they carried lice and other parasites. And on top of the biohazard conditions, the frigid cells probably helped combat all the bacteria and germs, but this miserable environment was pure, freezing hell.

I had some idea about what I was getting into because I'd stayed here and in similar facilities during the first nine weeks after my initial arrest. I'd come prepared wearing extra-warm clothing. Outside of the cold and bacteria, the noise alone was enough to make me go crazy. Throughout the day and night without stopping, inmates shouted, fought, and slammed doors. Shortly after I arrived, I found a space on the floor to lie down and rest. I closed my eyes, trying to get some rest while I processed what my next thirty months behind bars would look like. A few minutes later, I was awakened by the sting of fists raining down on my head. I opened my eyes to see a psychotic lunatic standing over me. He was either high, insane, or both. I sprang up from the concrete floor, slammed him against the wall, and started yelling for the guards to get him out of there. Not a great day one.

During my stay, Jackie would come to visit me each week. I at least had one good thing to look forward to. However, in these facilities, unlike federal prisons, inmates are not allowed in the same room with visitors. I had to speak with Jackie through a phone on the other side of a glass wall—just like all the movies and TV shows I'd seen. But now I was the bad guy in the jumpsuit sitting on the other side of the glass. That hurt the most.

After six weeks in that hellhole, I was finally transferred to FCI Safford, the federal prison where I'd be serving my time. They loaded twenty of us onto a stripped-down prison bus, fully shackled from our legs to our waist. Black boxes covered our arms so we couldn't move or make contact with other inmates. We all wore green jumpsuits because they used a color system to identify who was coming and going—green was for transfers.

After about an hour and a half, we arrived at FCI Safford. We exited the bus single file and shuffled our way through the gates.

Middle of the summer heat pounded down on us. Sweat streamed down my face, but it was a relief from the frozen cell I'd come from. Although the facility was covered in razor wire, I was surprised to see the facility was not a massive concrete complex like I imagined federal prison to be.

As we entered the gates, the guards removed our shackles and black boxes, placing them into milk crates for the next round of transfers. Then the guards handed us brown paper bags with our "lunch" for the day and escorted us into a large holding cell with wooden benches. We all sat there eating our lunches until they called our names in alphabetical order. I didn't have to sit too long before getting processed.

During processing, they photographed me, took my fingerprints, and issued my clothing—brown pants and a brown top that looked like medical scrubs (much better than the pink underwear with black and white stripes that Maricopa County issued). For shoes, they gave us black work boots and blue slip-ons, but once I got inside, I was surprised to find out I could buy new shoes, even big brands like Nike.

After processing, they transferred me to another holding cell to wait some more. Hurry up and wait is the name of the game in prison. By the time everyone was processed, it was getting late, and I was ready to be done. I needed sleep bad. Finally, they called my name and escorted me out of the holding facility. After exiting and entering multiple gates, I was in the prison yard.

Again, I was pleasantly surprised. The layout was not like the prison environment I'd expected. Inmates were housed in dormitories consisting of eight-person cubicles in one of two housing units. No isolated, barred prison cells. In the middle, between each dorm wing, is a dayroom and the bathrooms. The cafeteria and a recreation area were in a different area called "The Yard."

The violent and psychotic inmates I had to be wary of during my stay at CCA were not allowed here.

A guard led me to a cubicle that contained four bunks and showed me my bed. When I added all the cubicles and inmates up, it equated to sixty-four inmates having free access to one another. I wasn't sure how I felt about that coming out of my last experience, but I could sense the vibe was different. Nobody was shouting or fighting. The only noise I could hear was snoring and music—not ideal for sleeping, but it was better than getting awakened by fists pounding down on my head.

A lot of inmates had Walkman's they'd purchased in the commissary. Some would take a milk carton and put an earphone inside the carton to create a portable speaker. The night sounds blended to an orchestra of upbeat mariachi, hip-hop, heavy metal, and snores. I noted that my first purchase at the commissary would be earplugs, but I was too tired to care that first night. I fell asleep as soon as I closed my eyes. I slept better than I had in weeks.

FEWER CHOICES, BETTER RESULTS

The next morning at 5:00 a.m. a pudgy guard who looked like a human version of Porky Pig woke me up.

"Dunn, you're coming with me. Put on your boots."

He was with an internal department called the Construction Management System. I'd been assigned to a maintenance work crew, and work started on day one.

Before work began, I was led to the chow hall for breakfast. I didn't have high hopes coming from CCA where the best thing on the menu was powdered eggs, but I soon found out meals in federal prison were a major upgrade. It was buffet style with a cereal bar, oatmeal, pancakes, real eggs, and bacon—everything you could want and more. They even had salmon and lox!

I piled my plate up high, looking forward to eating real food for the first time in over a month, when a new problem presented itself: where to sit. Where I'd come from, everyone self-segregated. If you didn't sit with people who looked like you, you'd get a beating. I was still trying to figure out the "rules," so I sat by myself, close to the "woods," the term they called white guys. Segregation happened here, but it wasn't quite as distinct as it was in the state facility.

Breakfast was not social hour. We were told to eat fast, no bullshitting. We had a full day of work ahead of us. I was looking forward to it because for the past six weeks my only options were to lie in a bunk and stare at the ceiling or watch TV. My work crew had ten people, a mix of white guys, Native Americans, and Mexican Americans.

Porky Pig led us through some metal detectors and into a construction warehouse where we'd get assigned tools for the day. We had to exchange our prison IDs for the tools, and once we had our tools, we were responsible for returning them. I was issued a wheelbarrow. Some guys got wire cutters and tool belts. One guy got a machete. That got my attention. How were they giving a convict a machete? When I saw that, I realized my new environment was laxer from the one I'd just come from, but I remained wary.

The day's work consisted of repairing fences around the prison and some other miscellaneous maintenance. We got paid twenty-four cents an hour. It felt good to be working and building up a sweat. My mind and body were occupied doing something productive. I didn't have to think, just work, and the harder I worked, the better I felt.

Not everybody took my approach. Some of the guys didn't do anything. They just screwed around and collected their twenty-four cents. Other guys, like the crew boss Carlos, who was a South-Sider serving a twelve-year sentence, grinded hard every day. The hard workers became friends because we had a similar mindset. We had pride in our work and, more importantly, pride in ourselves. Working on the construction crew helped me form my first friendships in prison.

Most days I'd stop working around 3:00 p.m., then head back to my bunk and nap for a couple of hours until chow time. Dinner started at 6:00 p.m., and the yard stayed open until 9:00. After eating, I could do whatever I wanted, but still, my choices were extremely limited compared to the outside world. Some inmates chose to watch TV. I always avoided TV because I've never been a TV person, and more importantly, that area was a hotbed for fights. That's right, people fight in prison over which shows to watch, but the typical TV fights in prison escalate a lot more than the fights between a husband and wife.

At first glance, prison seemed like the ultimate removal of choice—when to eat, sleep, work, even what to wear was dictated to me. But as the days turned into weeks, I began to notice something unexpected. With so many decisions removed from my daily life, the choices that remained became clearer, more significant. Should I work hard on my crew or loaf around for twenty-four cents an hour? Should I watch TV where fights broke out regularly or spend my time lifting weights and improving myself? Should I hang out with guys still chasing highs or build relationships with people like Carlos who showed up every day ready to work? These weren't small daily decisions—they were choices about who I wanted to become.

After a few months, the prison launched construction on a new visitation center. A special crew took shape to tackle the project, and my strong work ethic over the past few months earned me a spot on the team. Carlos and another South-Sider, O.C., also joined the effort. We shifted from minor maintenance tasks to constructing something meaningful. The process energized me. Building the visitor center stirred excitement among the inmates, as it promised a space to reunite with loved ones. I poured my effort into a project that carried deep purpose, one that everyone regarded as a positive step forward. It felt amazing.

I remember one day, after a long day of pouring cement, I was walking through the yard covered in gray powder. I heard comments like, "Damn, Dunn, look at you." I was earning respect. People took notice. I was giving my peers something they wanted. I felt important. My nature had always been to make people happy, but now I was doing it in a positive way—a way that wouldn't end up hurting them or me. Good choices lead to better outcomes, and with all the distractions stripped away by the nature of the prison environment, I started to see how simple making a good choice could be.

The principles of how environment and choices work together remain the same inside or outside of prison. If you find yourself stuck in a cycle of making bad choices and feel like you can't get out, the first thing to do is take an honest hard look at your environment. But what makes an environment an environment? I learned the biggest factor in my transformation wasn't the restricted environment itself—it was the people I chose to surround myself with inside those walls.

YOUR ENVIRONMENT IS YOUR PEOPLE

The *Oxford English Dictionary* provides different definitions for the word "environment" depending on the context, and the one I'm speaking to is defined as follows: "The social, political, or cultural circumstances in which a person lives, especially with respect to their effect on behavior, attitudes, etc." When I think back to the environment I was living in before prison and look at the social and cultural conditions I surrounded myself with, and how that affected my behavior and attitude, I can clearly see how the people I chose to surround myself with created a toxic environment—one that limited my choices to mostly negative ones. I should note I also had a lot of good people in my life, but the negative influences always seemed to win. As a result, I'd end up disappointing the people I loved most.

It's funny to think that prison would be an upgrade to my environment, but because I chose to spend time with people striving to be something better, prison was a major upgrade to my environment. I formed friendships I still have to this day.

One evening at the weight pile, I met a dude who would help change my life: Robby Kesling. The first thing I thought when I saw Robby is *I hope I never get on this guy's wrong side.* He stands about six-foot-three, weighs 285 pounds, and is chiseled. He's a wrestler, a world champion in jujitsu, and a former University of Wyoming football player. Robby was serving a nineteen-year sentence for drug trafficking. I soon found out that Robby was looked upon as a leader among the other inmates, partly because of his intimidating size and combat skills, but probably more so because he was always trying to save people.

He was an incredible force of positivity. He grew up in the Alaskan bush hunting and fishing and living the roughneck life. He never really touched alcohol or did drugs, even when he was trafficking them. He's a purist in many ways, and I could see from the start this was a guy whom I wanted to hang and spend more time with.

Because Robby was an athlete and fitness guy, we hit it off right away. But the greatest gift Robby gave me was the encouragement to start taking college courses. FCI Safford offers courses to inmates through Eastern Arizona College. Robby told me about different courses they offered and introduced me to another great guy who was an instructor—Coach Jeff Roebuck. At the time, he was the defensive coordinator for the Eastern Arizona College football team. Three nights a week he'd come to FCI Safford and teach classes. I never planned on taking classes in prison, but this was a huge opportunity to accomplish my goal of making the most out of my time. Now I could walk out of the gates with an associate's degree. What an amazing opportunity to improve myself. I signed up right away. I aimed to get my associate's degree in business marketing. At the same time, I started teaching personal training classes to inmates through the encouragement of Robby.

I could feel my identity change. I was becoming the pure worker I'd always been, minus the contaminants. The best parts of me were shining brightest. All it took was changing my environment. Unfortunately for me, it took a drastic change in my environment before I could start making these life-changing connections. But it doesn't have to be that way for everyone. Sometimes knowing how to take the first step is enough to get the momentum you need to start changing your environment and your life.

THE THIRD CODE TO MIND OVER VIRTUALLY EVERYTHING:

Change your circle, change your life.

MOVE Sound Bite Summary

1. Your environment influences your choices, but you shape your environment through the people you choose to surround yourself with.

2. When you have fewer but better choices, making the right decisions becomes clearer and easier.

3. Your actions demonstrate the quality of your environment more than your words; who you spend time with shows who you're becoming.

4. Positive momentum builds when you surround yourself with people who are committed to growth and improvement.

5. Sometimes the path to a better environment requires accepting temporary discomfort.

CHAPTER 4

THE GLASS IS OVERFLOWING

"Instead of worrying about what you cannot control,
shift your energy to what you can create."
—Roy T. Bennett

"What's up? What are you guys having?"

I looked up from my seat at The Dirty Drummer to see a dark-haired, petite, tattooed bartender standing at our table. Something seemed different about her—not just her beauty, but an aura of confidence. My buddy Brian launched into his usual smooth talk, but she cut him off before he could finish.

"I don't care." She flashed a playful smirk. "What are you guys drinking?"

Most guys would have been discouraged by her sharp response. But watching her walk away, I turned to Brian and said, "I'm going to marry her."

He laughed, thinking I was joking. But I wasn't. Despite facing federal charges, despite all the uncertainty ahead, I felt something I hadn't felt in a long time—genuine optimism. Not just hope that things might work out, but a deep conviction that if I stayed focused on what I could control, I could turn my life around. Meeting Jackie made me believe in my future even more.

For me, the secret to getting through tough times has always been maintaining optimism. The *Oxford English Dictionary* defines optimism as follows: "(1) Hopefulness and confidence about the future or the successful outcome of something; (2) the belief that good must ultimately prevail over evil in the universe." You can see by these definitions that the concept of optimism is rooted in belief. It's very much a faith-based act; the idea of good overcoming evil is spiritual. But optimism is not just about passive belief. It's about fueling determination. It isn't simply expecting a good outcome. It's knowing that taking the right steps today will lead to a better tomorrow. Optimism provides the energy to keep moving forward, even when your circumstances are uncertain.

When life goes sideways and you find yourself in a dark place, you're ultimately left with two choices: Adopt a defeatist mindset and give up or adopt a winning mindset and accept the battle ahead, knowing the outcome is uncertain. A pessimistic person loses the war before the first battle begins. They never give themselves a chance. I know it's hard to fight when it feels like the odds are stacked against you, but the war isn't won in a single battle. Victory is achieved one battle at a time—sometimes over the span of years.

Optimism is a choice you have the freedom to make at any moment. But optimism alone is not enough. It must be paired with determination and action. Choosing optimism doesn't mean ignoring problems or hoping for a miracle. It means seeing the challenges ahead and deciding that you're willing to put in the work to overcome them. Optimism provides the mindset; determination provides the fuel.

JACKIE

That first night at The Dirty Drummer in September 2004 was just the beginning of the most important romantic relationship of my life. Brian's attempt at smooth talk had ended in flames, but Jackie's sharp dismissal only intrigued me more. She had fire. She was real—nothing like the superficial Scottsdale crowd I was used to. The girls I typically dated were all about appearances and status.

After a few rounds of drinks, we loosened up a bit and decided to take another shot. Brian took the lead again. This time his strategy was to throw me an assist.

"My friend Chad here is a sports trainer and rehab specialist. You look really fit, but you never know. You have any nagging injuries that need a professional touch?"

She played along. "Oh really? Well, let's see. I don't work out, but I do have a question. I have a hamstring injury from a car accident." She showed us a scar tissue mark on the back of her leg. "Can you make that go away or do anything to help?"

Now it was my turn. "I'm off the clock right now sweetie, but how about I give you my number and you can call me to discuss what I can do for you later." I wrote my number on a napkin and handed it to her. She took it, flashed a little smirk, and shoved the napkin into the back pocket of her cutoff jean shorts. "Perfect! I'll call you later," she said and walked away with our empty glasses.

My phone never rang.

I couldn't stop thinking about her, so I went back to The Dirty Drummer the next week. She remembered me, and this time without Brian by my side, the dynamic was different. The first thing that stood out was she didn't drink. A sober bartender. She said she didn't drink because she serves jackasses like me every day and sees what alcohol does to people. She really was all business. I thought that was badass.

Then I learned she was a single mother raising three children. For some men, after hearing that, they would have jumped off the barstool and walked out the door, never to return. But her kids didn't hit me as a negative. I saw it as an opportunity. She was single, and she needed someone. Why not me? Talking to her was easy; it felt good, and I wanted more.

Before I left that night I asked Jackie out. She said no. That became a pattern. For the next six months, I kept showing up, playing pool, and drinking just enough to justify being there. When I told her I was going to marry her, she said, "Get in line."

Most guys would have given up. But I wasn't chasing her for sport—I was proving I was serious. I asked about her life and what she wanted long-term. The more we talked Jackie saw I was different and genuine. I learned the names of her kids and always made a point to ask about them. "How's Chastin? How's Jade? How's Collin?" Another reason I kept coming, aside from wanting to get a date, was to protect her. Jackie is tough as nails, but working the night shift at a bar introduces risk for anyone. It's a scene filled with jackasses and knuckleheads of all types.

One night a rowdy drunk guy got out of line and was giving Jackie a hard time. After taking his drink away, she told him to leave several times, but he refused. He kept getting more belligerent, and the situation was escalating. I finally stepped in, and together, Jackie and I removed the guy. He threatened to return later after shooting a gun into the air. I stayed with Jackie through closing time to make sure nothing happened.

At the end of the night, she thanked me for staying and asked if I wanted to get an early breakfast. Finally, I'd broken through. This was my opportunity. But I had to be at work in six hours and needed sleep. I had to turn down her offer. How ironic, after all the time I'd put in just to have the chance. I went home and might as well have gone out with her because I tossed and turned all night thinking about her. However, I got my chance the next night. We had our first unofficial date at an IHOP the next morning at 2:30 a.m. after the bar closed.

After eating, we were sitting in my truck chatting, getting ready to head home. I thought if I was going to be with her, I needed to be honest from the start. I opened up my center console and pulled out my indictment for my federal case and handed it to her.

"Take a look at this. This is really who I am."

Jackie read the indictment in silence. I didn't know what to expect, but I was prepared for her to tell me she didn't want to have anything to do with me. When she finished reading it, she handed it back to me without saying anything.

"So?" I said.

"People make mistakes. That's life."

She didn't run away. She didn't reject me. She showed empathy. I knew by this time that she had all the characteristics I wanted in a life partner. She was an amazing mother, a hard-nosed worker, and had backbone. I needed a woman like her to put me in my place—somebody to tell me the truth, no matter how terrible it was, somebody to inspire me to be my best. Jackie was all of that and more. I felt like I had a winning lottery ticket in my hand. Unfortunately, it would be several years before I could cash it in.

From that point we continued to spend time together. I'd go see her at The Dirty Drummer, but I stopped drinking as much because

I no longer needed to justify my presence through that. Drinking also violated my pretrial release, so there was that too.

Eventually, she let me meet her kids—a major turning point. I knew then that Jackie trusted me. Her children are everything to her, so it was a risk for her to bring me into their lives. Because I'm a big kid at heart, they warmed right up to me. She could see from how they reacted to me and my genuine joy of spending time with them that she'd made the right choice. At the same time, she remained conflicted about our relationship. She knew she'd introduced her kids to a new father figure who wouldn't be around later.

There weren't any easy decisions for Jackie at the beginning of our relationship. She had to decide whether she wanted to commit to a guy like me with my criminal baggage. For me, the choice was clear as day—I wanted to be a family man, and I'd found my perfect partner and family. But I was going to prison and possibly for a long time. Whether Jackie would still want to be with me seemed mostly out of my hands. She could walk away at any moment, and nobody would think less of her, including me. The only thing I could do was be at peace and remain optimistic that she would still want to see me when I came out.

OPEN YOUR EYES: OPPORTUNITY IS ALL AROUND

Falling for Jackie taught me something crucial about optimism. It's not just about believing things will work out but about taking action even when the odds are stacked against you. I'd kept showing up at The Dirty Drummer not because I was certain of success, but because I saw a possibility where others might have seen rejection. Now, facing decades behind bars, I needed that same mindset more than ever. Just as I'd learned to see opportunity in a bartender's dismissal, I had to learn to see opportunity within prison walls.

The Bureau of Justice Statistics weren't in my favor. Within three years of release, about six in ten (62 percent) of people end up back behind bars.[1] But statistics don't determine individual outcomes. Choices do.

I knew that to avoid returning to prison after serving my time, I needed to do more than just not want to go back. Wanting wasn't enough. Hope alone wouldn't change anything. Optimism wasn't just about believing I could change. It was about committing to the actions that would make change real. Optimism gave me the vision of a better future, but determination made me build the foundation to get there. I started by changing my environment and spending time with positive-minded people who were also determined not to become another prison statistic. I also refused to adopt a victim mindset.

In prison I met two types of people: victims and the ones who take responsibility for their crimes. The victims focused on what was taken from them, what was unfair, and what they couldn't control. Early on I realized that optimism and taking responsibility for myself go hand in hand.

If I wanted a future outside these walls, I had to start believing I had the power to create it. Instead of dwelling on the unfairness of my circumstances, I focused on the opportunities I could seize: education, self-improvement, and preparing for the life I envisioned. Optimism isn't about ignoring the hardships; it's about refusing to let them dictate your story.

I quickly learned that prison has its own micro-economy with abundant opportunity, but only if you choose to see it that way. Many inmates saw only deprivation and limitation. In contrast,

---

[1] Bureau of Justice Statistics, "Recidivism of Prisoners Released in 34 States in 2012: A 5-Year Follow-Up Period (2012–2017)," date published July 2021, https://bjs.ojp.gov/library/publications/recidivism-prisoners-released-34-states-2012-5-year-follow-period-2012-2017.

my optimistic mindset helped me recognize possibilities everywhere I looked.

Take laundry, for example. Most inmates saw it as a dreaded two-hour chore, stuck in a crowded laundry room. I saw getting laundry done as an opportunity to build relationships and make life better for everyone involved. Five cans of tuna would get me my weekly laundry perfectly folded, bagged, and delivered to my bunk. For a couple more stamps or tuna cans, I could get my uniform pressed and looking sharp for visitor days. Instead of wasting time on laundry, I could focus on more valuable pursuits, like education and training. At the same time, I was helping other inmates develop marketable skills and a business sense they could use on the outside.

Different people brought different talents to prison, and many found ways to put those talents to work. The Native American inmates were exceptional craftsmen, turning simple materials into beautiful leather goods. I still remember the joy on Jade's face when I gave her the custom change purse they made—a great reminder that even in prison, we could create things of value and meaning.

For me, the obvious opportunity was in fitness training. I was certified and knew how to build strength and agility. While some might have seen working out as passing time, I saw it as a chance to help others transform their lives, just as I was transforming mine. The market for personal training was huge. Many guys wanted to get stronger, healthier, and change their lives. But it wasn't just about physical transformation. Every training session was my opportunity to mentor, encourage, and help someone believe in their own potential for change.

This optimistic approach to prison life didn't just make time pass easier. It prepared me for success on the outside. I was learning valuable lessons about entrepreneurship, relationship building, and creating value from limited resources. More importantly,

I was proving to myself that if you maintain the right mindset, you see opportunities everywhere, even in the most restrictive environments.

BE AT PEACE WITH WHAT YOU CANNOT CONTROL

The first year of my incarceration, Jackie came to visit me about once a month. The drive from Phoenix to Safford took nearly four hours one way. Her parents lived in Tucson, so she would drop the kids off with her parents on the way. Seeing Jackie, and sometimes the kids, was the thing I looked forward to the most. Unlike in CCA, I could be in the same room with Jackie at Safford with no glass wall separating us.

However, as the months went on, it started to wear her down. She was still working and taking on the duties of a single mother, so the long drive to visit me was taking an emotional toll on her. One day, on a phone call, she told me, "I can't do this anymore. I want to live my life, but I'll always be there for you. After your release, we'll find out if we're meant to be together."

At that moment, I faced the hardest test of my optimism. I had a choice to make—not just about how to react, but about how to think about the situation. The easy path would have been to sink into despair, to let circumstances dictate my mindset. Instead, I chose to see this challenge as another opportunity for growth. This wasn't about passively accepting her decision or hoping things would work out. It was about me actively choosing to believe in my own worth and potential, whether Jackie was part of my future or not.

I made the choice to cut off all communication—no phone calls, no letters, no contact. Not out of anger or defeat, but as a conscious choice to focus my energy on what I could control.

Up to this point, I'd been doing all of this to have the opportunity to be with her, to create a family with her. But now I had to choose a different path—one that didn't depend on any specific outcome.

I have to admit that at the time, this wasn't an instantaneous revelation for me. At first, I felt crushed, defeated, and depressed. I thought, *What have I been working so hard for?* My optimism had never been tested this much since I had arrived at Safford. Then something happened that snapped me out of my funk.

There had been some issues with my lawyer on my last DUI case. He hadn't filed some paperwork and didn't show up for my sentencing, which resulted in a new warrant being issued for me. I was already in prison, so the whole thing didn't make sense. After some back and forth with the courts, it was determined that everything could get sorted out if I went to superior court and back to the Maricopa County jail, also known as the Towers Jail complex. Up to this point, life behind bars was going better than I ever imagined, but now I had to go back to county jail, the worst place anyone can serve time. On top of Jackie being out of my life, it suddenly felt like I was moving backward.

My time at Towers Jail was worse than I could have imagined. Within days, I had a cellmate's colostomy bag explode on my bunk and drip all over my feet, a fitting start to my time there. County jail isn't only about punishment; it's about survival. There's no sunlight, no structure, and no respect among inmates. It's pure chaos.

One day, some guys decided to clog the toilets in protest, flooding the entire jail. Guards responded with a full lockdown, stripping us to our boxers, tossing our cells, and leaving us in freezing conditions. That was the lowest of the low for me.

At Towers Jail, I fell back into survival mode, seeing one disaster after another. When you're in conditions like that, there's no headspace for reflection or rehabilitation. You're just trying to endure each day without losing your mind. During my time at Towers Jail,

I realized prison had changed me. A year earlier, I might have fed into the anger, the victim mentality, the chaos. But now, I knew the only way forward would be to stay in control of myself, no matter how bad the environment. I wouldn't let this place break me.

Finally, after six weeks, my stay at Towers Jail ended. I got the notice that I'd be transferred back to Safford. They'd finally come to get me. I handed in my black-and-white striped jumpsuit and pink boxers. "Thank God," I thought. I never wanted to step foot inside that place again.

Although six weeks in Towers Jail tested my optimism in ways I never expected, I discovered something new: Optimism isn't just a feeling; it's a practice. Every morning in that hellhole, I made an active choice to find something worth working toward. When my cellmate's colostomy bag exploded on my bunk, I chose to see it as a reminder of why I never wanted to return to jail. When other inmates protested by flooding the toilets, I chose to focus on maintaining my own standards, my own dignity.

This is what I mean by active optimism—it's not about pretending everything is fine or passively hoping for the best. It's about consciously choosing to find opportunity in adversity, about taking action to create better outcomes even in the worst circumstances. Every day in Towers I made a choice between letting the environment break me or using it to make me stronger.

During my final months at Safford, I noticed another change taking place in my mindset. I started tuning out the noise. Instead of hearing, I began to focus on seeing. I started to visualize what life would be like for me after prison—not just with Jackie, but also without her. That was a turning point because I stopped basing my future on whether she would still be waiting for me or not. I stopped thinking in terms of what I had lost and started thinking about what I was becoming. I knew I had everything I needed to build a life of value—because that truth came from me. I learned that life isn't about waiting for someone to believe in you. It's about believing in yourself so fully that, no matter who stays or who leaves, you stay on your path.

One night before the yard locked down, I walked out to the prison track and sat down on the cement bleachers. I could see the stars flickering off in the distance and shining down over the desert beyond the prison walls. I thought about the open and free space of the wilderness filled with danger: snakes, tarantulas, coyotes. But the wilderness is also unrestrained. Whatever lived in the wilderness—animals or plants—found ways not only to survive but to thrive in the harshest environments.

Sitting there that night in silence, something came over me that I hadn't felt up to that point. It wasn't a feeling of want, it was a feeling of expectation. It was a decision I brought into my conscious mind. I knew, with every fiber in my body, prison was a place I would never return to. No matter what happened, Jackie or no Jackie, I would never do anything again to jeopardize my freedom. I had too much to give to the world. Prison had done what it was designed to do—punish people so they would turn their life around. I was thankful for that, but I was ready to go home.

THE LONG GOODBYE

My remaining six months at Safford flew by. We finished building the visitor center and broke ground on a new dormitory. My friendship with Robby and some other guys kept growing stronger, and we continued to motivate each other. I completed my coursework and got my associate's degree, and because I'd managed to stay out of trouble, I got my early release.

When you're released from prison, if you've made friends, you get a little going away party the night before. I'd made friends, incredible friends, so the night before my release I got my party.

We all met up in a common area where we played cards every night. The guys had made us all bagel sandwiches and a prison cake out of some pastries. It was badass. I could feel these guys really cared about me. Along with food, there's another important tradition of a prison goodbye that includes physical pain. Your buddies send you off with some special bruises. I knew about this and was waiting for it to go down.

We had about thirty minutes left before the yard locked down for the night. I knew what was coming, so I got up from my card table. I wasn't going to make it easy on them. As soon as they saw me get up, they all came for me from different angles. The blanket we put on top of the metal was ripped off, and cards flew everywhere, and the next thing I knew, I was on the ground with about five guys on top of me. My arms were pinned down, and I was getting punched in the legs, one dead leg after another. That's where they target you, so they don't do any major damage. The end result is numb legs and some big bruises.

You're probably thinking this sounds like a nightmare. It is. That's the point. It's supposed to hurt and serve as a reminder to not return. It's tough love. The message: "We love you, but we never want to see you in here again." They all said that to me too. "We love you, brother, but don't come back."

After everyone got off me, I stayed lying on the floor with tears in my eyes. I wasn't crying from pain, though. I was crying because this was goodbye, and I don't like goodbyes. Just like I'd cry every time Jackie said goodbye, it was happening again. I knew I'd be leaving the greatest friends I'd ever had in life, and it hurt.

The next morning, Robby and Lance walked me to processing.

"I've never seen anyone cry leaving prison," Robby said. "Only when they get here."

I wasn't crying because I was leaving. I was crying because I wasn't coming back.

When you leave prison, you have to be released to somebody. They don't just let you walk out of the gates and reenter the free world. You're still a prisoner in a sense. Originally, Jackie had planned to be there for me, but after we cut off contact, I asked my parents to come.

On April 16, 2008, my parents arrived around 10:00 a.m. to receive me. From the time of release, I had six hours to check in at the halfway house. On the way home, we first stopped at Circle K and bought a Thirst Buster Mountain Dew. I sipped on that for the next four hours as we made our way back to Phoenix. I still had two hours to burn, so I asked my parents to stop at The Dirty Drummer, hoping Jackie would be working.

When I stepped inside, it took a moment for my eyes to adjust. And there Jackie stood, her back turned, working the grill, unaware that everything was about to change in both our lives.

She turned. Our eyes met. Neither of us moved at first. Then she ran toward me. That hug said everything—more than words ever could.

That night, she visited me at the halfway house. We talked for two hours, but it felt like two minutes. Before she left, she handed me a small box. Inside was a brand-new phone.

"I thought you might need this."

Eight months of silence. An uncertain future, and now, in my hands, she'd given me a simple object that carried a bigger message: My optimism had paid off. I hadn't just hoped for a second chance. I had begun rebuilding myself and my life in a way that made a future with Jackie possible.

I walked into prison believing my future depended on things I couldn't control. I walked out knowing that optimism isn't just about waiting for things to get better—it's about doing the things you need to do to make them better.

Looking back now, I can see how every choice I made in prison—from throwing myself into work crews to pursuing education, from building legitimate enterprises to maintaining my standards in Towers Jail—wasn't about passing time. With each decision, I laid down another brick in the foundation of my future. While others waited for their time to pass, I chose to use time as a tool for my transformation. That's what real optimism looks like— not just by believing in better days ahead but by actively creating them through daily choices and consistent action.

The cell phone Jackie gave me wasn't only a means of communication. It symbolized the connection I'd maintained with her by choosing optimism over despair, growth over stagnation, action over acceptance. In prison, I'd learned that the glass isn't half full or half empty—it comes with unlimited refills. Every day presents new opportunities to fill your glass if you maintain the mindset to see those opportunities and seize them.

THE FOURTH CODE TO MIND OVER VIRTUALLY EVERYTHING:

Adopting an optimistic mindset is the best strategy for overcoming adversity and discovering new opportunities.

MOVE Sound Bite Summary

1. True optimism isn't passive hope. It's the active choice to find opportunities in every situation.

2. Optimism, paired with determination, transforms challenges into stepping-stones for growth and change.

3. An optimistic mind focuses on what it can control rather than dwelling on what it can't.

4. Optimism means taking responsibility for your future rather than viewing yourself as a victim of circumstances.

5. The power of optimism lies not in believing things will work out, but in believing in your ability to make things work out through consistent action.

CHAPTER 5

ONE IN A ROW

"A Journey of a thousand miles begins with a single step."
—Lao Tzu

"Just one step, Eddy. That's all we're thinking about right now."

I stood beside Eddy King, my hands hovering near his hips as he gripped the Swiss-ball rack that was mounted to the wall. Sweat beaded on his forehead. His legendary quads—those that powered him to BMX fame—trembled with effort. Doctors stated his chances of walking again after the accident were slim. But here he was, defying those predictions one painful movement at a time.

"One step," Eddy repeated, his voice tight with concentration. We'd been at this for weeks, reprogramming his brain to remember what his legs had once known instinctively. The first time we tried,

I had to physically move his legs for him. Now he was doing it himself—not yet walking but fighting for that crucial first step.

His right leg inched forward, shaking but holding. The movement was small, barely noticeable to anyone watching, but to us, it was *everything*. One step. One victory. One moment that would lead to another, and another, until eventually, Eddy would not only walk again but return to the bike that had made him a legend.

That single step taught me more about success than all my years of training combined. It wasn't just about rehabilitation or physical therapy. It was about the power of breaking down seemingly impossible goals into their smallest components. I learned this philosophy from my dear friend and legendary basketball coach Art Dye. He would tell his players that to become a great shooter, you have to start by making one shot in a row.

At first thought, doing one small thing at a time seems almost too simple. But within that simplicity lies a powerful truth about how lasting change happens. Whether you're learning to walk again after a devastating injury, rebuilding your life after prison, or chasing a seemingly impossible dream, success comes down to focusing on one step, one shot, one moment at a time.

THE FIRST STEP TO FREEDOM

When you get released from prison, your next stop is a "halfway house," or residential facility designed to help people transition from prison life back into society. They're also used for people exiting rehab programs. A halfway house provides a stable, supportive setting where residents can learn life skills, find employment, and receive counseling or treatment as needed. Halfway houses have strict rules, including a curfew. As valuable as halfway houses are, for me this transitional house was a pain in my ass. I knew I was rehabilitated and ready to change my life, but instead of going home and starting that new life, I still felt like a prisoner, despite being gainfully employed at Rehab Plus and scheduled to start working there the day after my release.

I had to stay at the halfway house for six weeks before I could go back to my parents' home. The worst part of the experience was my roommate. He had also come out of prison, but he either never followed the prison code of respect, or he decided he no longer needed to follow that code. He had a bad habit of talking on the phone and playing his music late at night, making my sleep nearly impossible. This roomie acted like I wasn't even in the room. Zero respect. Eventually I had some heated conversations with him, which helped a little, but he continued to test my patience. I wasn't about to go back to prison for beating this guy up, so I did my best to get through it, one day at a time.

On top of the halfway house troubles, I was also hit with five years of probation. I was required to hand in my monthly bank statements, get permission for any purchases over $500, and submit a daily drug test for the first six months. The daily drug tests had to be administered at the downtown federal court building, but my license was still suspended for another year and a half, so I'd either have to take public transportation or get a ride from Jackie, friends, or family.

As thankful as I was to be out of prison, in many ways, getting through the early part of post-prison life was more difficult. I felt amped up and ready to be a hard-nosed, honest worker to become the man Jackie and the kids needed. But I was still hamstrung by my past. I had to depend on people to help me, and I hated it. I was supposed to be helping them! My optimism got put to the test again.

I stayed committed to grinding every day and eventually was released from the halfway house. Getting out of that place was a big relief, but I still had to deal with probation and all its restrictions and inconveniences. My relationship with Jackie got off to a good start, and I could stay with her some nights after getting approval from my probation officer. Work was also going well. It felt amazing to finally be moving in the right direction again.

After four weeks of living with my parents, I got my probation switched so I could go live with Jackie, her roommate, and the kids. We built our love and relationship one day at a time, one trip to work after another. Time together was the driving force, but that could be good or bad, especially as she just got me back into her schedule. I needed Jackie, but the reality of the situation was in many ways I was more of a fourth kid than a partner carrying half the weight.

The grind was real. Getting the kids ready early for school so Jackie could drive me thirty minutes to be at work at 7:00 a.m. Then she'd turn around and drive thirty minutes back to Mesa to drop off the kids at two separate schools. All in the a.m. traffic. Then we both went to work—I needed to make money as I rebuilt my new life, and she worked her ass off to raise three kids under eight years old. She then went to the day care right after work and picked the kids up and headed to Phoenix to pick me up at 7:00 p.m. from Rehab Plus. Dinner at 8:30, homework, baths, and bed. Wake up and repeat!

BECOMING A FAMILY MAN

Despite our struggles, I stayed committed to realizing my vision of becoming a family man. I knew that building the family I wanted would happen one small victory at a time. I couldn't rush the process. I was determined to be the strong husband Jackie deserved and the loving father the kids needed, but I had to tackle each obstacle as it came—one day, one challenge, one conscious choice at a time.

Living the "one in a row" philosophy meant celebrating each tiny step toward becoming the man Jackie and her children needed. Some days that victory was simply making it to work on time. Other days it was having enough energy after a long day to help with homework. Each small win built on the last, creating a foundation for something greater.

During this time together, Jackie told me, "I want to get married before I turn thirty." I filed that piece of information away. Just as I was learning with my clients at Rehab Plus, you don't tackle the biggest challenge first—you start with what's achievable today, then build toward the larger goal tomorrow.

My original elaborate proposal plan was to fly her out to San Diego and ask her to discover different clues throughout the day, culminating with me kneeling on the sand in front of the ocean asking for her hand in marriage. When I told Jackie's friend about my brilliant idea, she said, "Jackie's not going to do that."

"Why not?" I asked.

"Jackie doesn't fly, and she's not leaving her kids."

That ended that romantic idea—another lesson in the importance of taking the right step at the right time, not just any step forward.

My actual proposal ended up being less romantic and more in line with who Jackie and I are. We were at the mall walking around, and we passed a jewelry store. I suggested we pop in for a second and look at rings. I wanted to get a sense of what kind of ring Jackie would like. No surprise to me, she chose a simple ring, tried it on, and it looked great.

"What's it cost?" I asked the sales lady.

"$2,500."

"Not bad," I thought. Originally, I'd planned to spend much more, so being a man of action and seeing an opportunity, I got down on my knee and proposed to Jackie right there at the jewelry store.

I had a plan to make payments in the amount of $450, which would not need approval by my probation officer. I knew I could afford the payments, and this would allow me to stay within the restrictions while still giving Jackie the ring she deserved.

"Jackie, will you be my wife?"

She looked shell-shocked. After collecting herself, she smiled and said, "Sure!"

I didn't know for sure if Jackie really wanted to marry me, but I received the answer I wanted from her. That single "Sure!" represented a major milestone on my path to becoming a family man. I also felt confident we'd make it work and signed up for a store credit card to buy the ring. We celebrated that night by going out to dinner at The Cheesecake Factory. When we returned home, I anticipated a sensual night in the bedroom to cap off our engagement day. Instead, Jackie was laid up with food poisoning—not the storybook start to our family that I'd imagined, but I had taken a massive step closer to getting the thing I wanted most. It was a restless night of sleep next to my suffering future wife, but life was good, and I knew it.

The road to building a family wasn't without setbacks. Like physical rehabilitation, moments of progress were followed by painful regressions. After I'd collected some paychecks, I finally got myself in a position to give something back by pitching in for a new couch for the house. Just as I was gaining momentum, I hit an obstacle: The couch cost more than $500, so I had to ask my probation officer for permission to buy it. She denied it, telling me, "That's an unnecessary purchase." Another reminder I was a long way from the type of freedom I wanted, but I kept moving forward, one small victory at a time.

The restraints of my release continually tested Jackie's patience. When you're on probation, your probation officer can make surprise visits to see if you're meeting the terms of your release. One day, for some reason, my probation officer thought it would be appropriate to do a three o'clock in the morning check-in. Naturally, we were all asleep. The loud knocking woke Jackie, and she answered the door.

The probation officer entered the house and turned on the lights in every bedroom, including the kids' rooms. Jackie doesn't stand for anyone causing her kids distress, so that incident pushed the limits of her patience. But what broke the camel's back was when I got jealous because a guy I didn't know texted Jackie, so I called an old girlfriend to make Jackie feel jealous. That bad choice resulted in me getting the boot—a painful reminder that one step backward can undo multiple steps forward.

A few weeks after I'd moved back in with my parents, I got a call from Jackie. Her daughter Jade's birthday party was coming up, and she had asked Jackie if I could be there. She knew Jade really wanted to see me, so she allowed it. This invitation, though small, felt like my first step back toward the family I longed for.

The party was a success, and it felt amazing being back with Jackie and the kids. The time away had given Jackie the space she needed to think. I hoped I proved that despite all the baggage I was bringing, the net positive effect of having me in the house outweighed the inconveniences. I wanted to be there for Jackie and the kids. We had a long conversation that night after Jade's party, and we reconciled. I was back in the picture and had another shot to become a family man.

I didn't move back in right away. We took it slow, applying the "one in a row" philosophy to our relationship. One good conversation led to one positive interaction with the kids, which led to us spending more quality time together, which continued over the span of months as we strengthened our trust and bond. I focused on better communication and did my best to be the man Jackie needed, rather than an immature child—the one thing she needed the least. Each day, I made a conscious choice to be better than I was the day before.

After getting a second chance to be with the family I wanted, I was determined to not give Jackie any reasons to pull away again. We were married on the beach in Coronado, California, on September 12, 2009, fourteen months after our engagement. Jackie had always wanted a beach wedding, so we made it happen. We drove there, of course. Jackie's oldest son Collin was my best man, Jade was one of the flower girls, and our little man Chastin was the ring bearer. The wedding party was small on both sides, but both Jackie and I had some of our closest friends there with us.

After the wedding, we had one day to spend at the beach. Then we went right back to work. No honeymoon for us. I had to get permission from my probation officer to leave the state of Arizona. Outside of that hassle, we had three kids to take care of with a meager income, so we went straight back to the daily grind. Building a family isn't about grand gestures. It's about showing up every day, making one right choice after another, stringing together small victories until they compound into something beautiful.

The first two years of our marriage consisted of the same struggles new couples have when adjusting to married life. Instead of continuing to date each other, we put all our energy into taking care of the kids and working. Over the next eight years at Rehab Plus, I only took four days off. By marrying Jackie, I'd become the family man I'd always dreamed of, but I wanted more than a continual grind for myself and my new family. Just as a physical therapy patient must move beyond basic function toward thriving, I knew I had more to give, but I didn't yet know what, until I met some special people at Rehab Plus who would teach me even more about taking life one step at a time.

EDDY KING: THE POWER OF BELIEF

When Eddy first wheeled into Rehab Plus, he brought a quality with him I recognized immediately: unshakable belief. His doctors told him, "You might never walk again." Eddy's response? "You don't know who you're working with." Eddy's unshakable belief in himself, which might sound like arrogance to some, is the kind of belief that makes the impossible possible.

Before I started working with Eddy, I came across a story about him on my Facebook timeline. I recognized the name right away because Eddy King is a BMX racing legend. The story detailed a recent bike accident that had left him paralyzed from the waist down. The shock pump from his hydration pack had crushed his T11 and T12 vertebrae. Eddy was a hero of mine, so I dug a little deeper and found a way to reach him through a Cambridge Medical website post asking for support for Eddy's recovery.

I decided to throw my fishing pole in the water and sent him a message. "Hey Eddy, this is Chad Dunn out in Arizona. I used to race BMX bikes. If you ever have the chance to get out to Arizona, I'd love to work with you and help you battle back from your spinal cord injury." I'd never worked with a spinal cord injury before, but I knew I could help him. I just didn't know how; I'd figure that out later.

Two months had passed when a message from Eddy popped up in my inbox. "Hey Chad, my mom lives in Arizona. I'll be moving there in a month. Let's hook up. I'd love to see if you can help me."

I reread the message a couple times to make sure I was reading it correctly. I couldn't believe it. I was about to get the chance to work with one of my heroes.

The day after arriving in Arizona, Eddy wheeled himself through the doors of Rehab Plus. He'd shown up just as he said. Now reality for me set in. I didn't know if Warren and Mitch, our physical therapists and the owners of Rehab Plus, would allow me to work with him, but I'd brought him into the business after all. I hoped they'd give me a shot. I wanted to work with Eddy the most of any of the famous athletes I'd worked with over the years. Helping a BMX Hall of Famer and pioneer of the sport became an opportunity I knew I'd never have again. The nature of his injury would give me valuable experience to help further my craft.

When I started working with Eddy, right away I could see we were going to figure this thing out as a team. He'd already put in a lot of self-education and had made some progress with his recovery. Not having all the pressure on me to perform a miracle felt like a relief. A realist from day one, Eddy set the tone: "I've learned every spinal cord injury is different, so you really have to be self-taught through trial and error." That insight gave me more confidence because that was my plan anyway. Plus, I'd already learned for myself working with clients that what works for one person isn't necessarily going to work for another.

We started out by placing electrical stimulation on Eddy's legs to get the muscles firing. After that, I got him on a stationary bike where Eddy felt most comfortable. Because Rehab Plus isn't set up for spinal cord rehab, I had to get creative. I couldn't just put him through the standardized protocols we'd established for our typical sports injury patients. What Eddy needed most was just to *move*, however we could accomplish that.

I'd do things like tie him up to straps and get him leaning into space for balance. Sometimes that went well, sometimes it didn't. Every night after work, I'd go home to research and strategize for our next session. Although he was paralyzed from the waist down, Eddy's quads still fired, so I knew we could get him to at least support his own weight and possibly walk.

After only a couple sessions, Eddy could support himself with a walker. Next thing was to get him to take his first step. I'd take his right leg in my hands and move it forward for him. Then I'd take his left leg and move it forward to match the right leg. We needed to retrain his brain to know what the motions felt like to reset the pathways. We were literally practicing the "one in a row" philosophy Coach Dye had talked about.

Eddy and I kept grinding like this for many weeks, one step at a time. Finally, Eddy took his first step without the assistance of a walker. "There you go, man, you did it. You walked!"

"I didn't walk, bro. I took a couple of steps."

That's Eddy.

Watching Eddy reclaim his mobility, one tiny movement at a time, shifted my entire perspective on progress. Although his physical progress was remarkable, Eddy and I recognized that every small victory rewired both his body and his mind. When Eddy first supported his own weight with a walker, I saw him light up with renewed determination. That single moment of success created momentum that carried into the next challenge and the next. I began to understand that "one in a row" wasn't just about breaking down big goals. It was about building belief through proof of progress.

Eddy's journey from paralysis to walking again had shown me the power of belief in driving recovery. But working with Anthony Ramos, my next challenge, tested the limits of what a person's belief and determination could overcome. While Eddy fought to regain movement in his legs, Anthony faced a different battle: learning to live in a body that had been transformed by fire.

ANTHONY RAMOS: FINDING FOCUS THROUGH FEAR

If Eddy taught me about belief, Anthony's journey showed me the true meaning of focus. When you've been burned over 70 percent of your body, every movement brings pain. Your natural instinct is to avoid it. But Anthony learned to focus beyond the pain, to see each small movement as progress rather than punishment.

Anthony Ramos was off-loading motor oil from a tanker onto a semitruck in Central Phoenix when the oil caught fire and sparked a massive blaze that engulfed his entire body. The flames from the fire shot over one hundred feet in the air. People could see the massive plume of black smoke for miles. Sky Harbor International Airport even had to temporarily suspend flights.

Fire engulfed Anthony's body for nearly three minutes before his partner pulled him to safety and tamped out the flames. Only one ambulance could access Anthony and his partner amid the chaos as fire crews fought to put out the massive fire, so both men had to be hauled out in the same ambulance. Anthony was propped up in a chair in back. Still conscious at that point, Anthony remembers looking down at his chest and watching massive swathes of his skin slide off his body and fall at his feet.

Because of his severe burns, doctors put Anthony into a medically induced coma for eleven weeks. A former intern at Rehab Plus named Danika was working at the Arizona Burn Center during that time, and after Anthony was stable enough to come out of the coma, she recommended that he go to Rehab Plus and work with us. She knew he needed somebody to help him with the mental side of his recovery.

I'd been working with Eddy for about four months and had steadily been building a reputation as what I felt was "the mental guy."

If somebody was mentally struggling, I wanted them. If the injury was catastrophic, that was mine. A new identity was emerging for me, and not only did I love it; I was really good at it. When Danika told me about Anthony, I had never worked with a burn victim before, and even though his case was about as bad as they come, I didn't hesitate to tell her to send him over. For me, it was a new challenge, and I was starving for new challenges.

When Anthony arrived at Rehab Plus, I didn't do the tissue work, but I did all the exercise activities—everything that required motivation and positive energy to get through. I became Anthony's biggest cheerleader and put everything I had into building him up mentally and rebuilding his confidence. "Good work, Anthony! You flexed your knees ninety degrees today. Tomorrow we're going to get ninety-one degrees!" Once again, we were practicing the "one in a row" philosophy.

Not every day was a win for Anthony as he fought to heal. The most important part of Anthony's recovery was the positive environment at Rehab Plus. Not only did he have us encouraging him, but Eddy was still there, working through his recovery. Eddy always wore a shirt with one word written on the back that encapsulated everything we were doing: "Believe." I knew from my prison experience believing was the key to moving forward. Working with Eddy had confirmed it.

For burn victims, it's especially critical to never stop progress. They're in a constant battle against their damaged skin, scarring up and restricting their movement. They endure ongoing surgeries to cut this scar tissue that enables them to move. It's a torturous recovery and the toughest recovery mentally. Burn survivors must fight daily to keep doing something that causes them pain, even though the pain will pay off for them in the future.

One day Anthony told me something that perfectly captured his mental struggle.

"You want to feel like a piece of shit?" Anthony asked me. "Go to the gas station with your wife and sit in the car while she pumps the gas."

Although Anthony was physically capable of pumping the gas, he suffered from post-traumatic stress disorder. The last time he had a flammable hose in his hand, he almost died. After hearing how humiliated Anthony felt about his state of mind, I realized the gravity of our work together to deal with both his physical and mental state.

Part of Anthony's recovery became pumping his own gas again. I told him he had to face his fear to overcome it, but he hesitated to take on the task at first. A few weeks later, I got a text message from him with a video he'd taken using his phone. I could see Anthony's hand on the gas pump and how he successfully put the pump in the tank, pulled the handle, and set the automatic lock tab so it would fill up without him having to keep holding the handle. Halfway through the video, the automatic lock tab popped off, and he dropped his phone. That scared the shit out of him! We both laughed about it when I saw him at the next session. Even though he didn't pump the gas perfectly, facing and overcoming this fear became a big moment in Anthony's recovery.

Anthony's journey with the gas pump also revealed another dimension of the "one in a row" philosophy I hadn't fully grasped before. Sometimes one victory isn't about physical progress at all. It's about conquering fear. That video of him gripping the pump handle, though it ended with him dropping his phone in panic, represented more than just facing his fears. It showed me how breaking through mental barriers often requires the same incremental approach as physical rehabilitation. You don't conquer fear in one grand gesture. You chip away at it, one small brave act at a time.

Another milestone for Anthony happened at home when his wife left him with their baby boy to go grocery shopping. When his child got his arm stuck in the slats of the crib, he started crying in distress. At the time, Anthony's still bandaged arms restricted his ability to move, but he knew he had to get his baby's arm free.

"I don't know how I did it, Chad, but I was able to reach into the crib, free my baby's arm from the slat, and pull him up into my arms. That was the first time I'd held him since my accident." What a lesson in courage and determination!

The most impactful story I remember about Anthony happened at the tail end of our time together. It reminded me I was doing meaningful work and truly changing people's lives. After I worked with Anthony for almost four years, he and his family decided to move to Texas. Shortly after his move, Anthony's former landlord called to tell him that he'd found a handgun on the top of the refrigerator.

Because Anthony had already moved to Texas, he called me to ask if I could get the gun for him and ship it. Due to my charges, I couldn't mess with the gun, so Jackie took it to the gun shop to be mailed. Anthony told me later that he'd placed the gun there because, at one time, he had considered suicide. I knew then how far Anthony had come. I also felt immense pride knowing that I had been instrumental in helping him get his life back.

Working with Anthony deepened my understanding of how mental and physical recovery intertwine. His triumph at the gas pump and freeing his baby boy proved that sometimes the biggest victories happen far from the gym. Ultimately, I had helped Anthony, but he'd helped me just as much, whether he knew it or not.

PHILLIP GRIGG: THE HEART OF CONSISTENCY

Phillip Grigg, another client of mine, demonstrated what consistency really means. As a posse member of the Maricopa County

Sheriff's Office, he had literally taken a bullet trying to help others. Working with him showed me how the "one in a row" philosophy could rebuild not just a body, but an entire life.

On New Year's Eve 2013, Phil's life changed forever when a vehicle struck his pickup truck as he drove home from Walgreens. The driver was fleeing from the scene of an armed robbery outside an IHOP restaurant. The officer pursuing him watched as the suspect collided with Phil.

Right after the collision, the on-duty police officer attempted to apprehend the driver, but the suspect put up a fight. Phil saw the struggle and stepped in to aid the officer, but the suspect, a mountain of a man, stood six-and-a-half feet tall and weighed more than 250 pounds. Both Phil and the officer struggled to detain him. During the struggle, the man managed to pull the officer's gun away from him and shoot that policeman in the hip and Phil in the gut.

Both Phil and the officer survived, but the bullet blasted through Phil's side and obliterated his stomach. It punctured Phil's liver in two different places and split his kidney in half. Phil's prognosis was grim. He almost bled out on the scene and was lucky to be alive. Doctors treated him in the ICU for six months. For the first three months, Phil was in a coma. During his recovery, he also battled sepsis and even clinically died a couple times.

After losing half his body weight, Phil could easily have given up. Instead, he showed up to rehab with me every day, pushing a little further than the day before. Even when he could barely last ten minutes on the elliptical, he came back the next day, ready for more. Phil's story hit especially close to home for me because I knew Phil. His wife, Betsy, was one of our patients at Rehab Plus, recovering from a total knee replacement.

A native West Virginian, Phil reminded me of Barney Fife from *The Andy Griffith Show*, and Mater, the tow truck from the Pixar animation film *Cars*. He was a Southern gentleman, full of life and personality. He had also flown helicopters during the Vietnam War. Before his accident, every time Phil came to Rehab Plus with Betsy, he brought infectious positive energy and held court. After his accident, this man whom I'd come to know and admire was in the fight of his life. I knew I had to help him when he felt ready.

His first day at Rehab Plus lasted about ten minutes. After losing 50 percent of his weight during the prior six months, he was basically starting to build back his body from ground-zero strength. I put him on the elliptical for about two minutes. Then I had him do some shoulder presses with negative weight—that's how weak he was. I quickly learned that Phil didn't back down from a fight. He showed up the next day and demanded I put some weight on the press this time. I knew then he would be just fine.

His doctor gave Phil a thirty-pound weight restriction for lifting to avoid a surgically induced hernia. His stomach had been reconstructed with pig skin. Despite these physical challenges, Phil showed up and did the work every day with a positive attitude. About four months into his recovery, Phil had worked his way up to thirty pounds and was pulling seated rows without any strain.

"Crank that baby up to sixty," he told me.

"Phil, I appreciate your drive, but you know you're restricted to thirty pounds."

"That's in each hand," he claimed.

I couldn't stop Phil from exceeding his thirty-pound weight restriction. From experience, I knew enough to know that patients usually know what they're capable of, so I changed the weight to sixty pounds, and Phil lifted that weight with no problem.

Phil's determination to increase his workload, even when starting from almost nothing, exemplified the compound effect of small, consistent efforts. Watching him progress from barely managing ten minutes on the elliptical to eventually exceeding his weight restrictions taught me that the "one in a row" philosophy isn't just about taking small steps—it's about trusting that those steps, however tiny they might seem in the moment, are building toward something bigger. Each small victory creates a foundation for the next challenge.

Phil was unstoppable. I can't remember one day of him showing an ounce of pessimism. The only time I ever saw Phil become emotional was after spending a year and a half in therapy and he got released to go back to work as a truck driver. "I finally got my life back," he said. "I get to do what I love again."

BECOMING THE PHYSICAL AND MENTAL GUY

Anthony, Eddy, and Phil became what I called "my three wise men." By working with them, I took the next step in my own evolution to become someone who could help our clients deal with their physical injuries and their mindsets. I'd always been known as the physical guy with high energy and positivity. Through my success with the three wise men, I learned I also had a natural gift for helping people mentally.

My time with Phil culminated in me returning to jail. However, I didn't go back to jail because I'd done anything wrong (thank goodness!). Instead, my old "friend" Maricopa County Sheriff Joe Arpaio had not only helped Phil during his recovery with donations, but he was also behind Phil receiving a Carnegie Medal, a national award for bravery. After Phil received the award, the local ABC News station contacted him for a story that would air during Thanksgiving. They wanted to interview him. Thinking of the business and the publicity it could bring, I told Phil, "Great! Let's do the interview at Rehab Plus."

"No," he said. "I want to do it at the sheriff's station, and I want you there with me." Phil didn't know I was a convicted felon. In fact, none of my clients knew it, and I preferred it that way, so I kept my mouth shut and agreed to go, despite not feeling pumped about the prospect of returning to jail under any circumstances.

The sheriff's office was in the same complex as Towers Jail, the place where I spent the most miserable six weeks of my life. The experience felt surreal since I was now going back to jail as a good guy, not a bad guy. There I sat in the heart of the criminal justice system as a special guest for a Carnegie Medal winner. Guests, reporters, and cameras packed the media room. Phil and I sat side by side on stage, a sheriff's posse member and a convicted felon.

Standing in the sheriff's office earlier that day—me, a former convict, beside Phil, a decorated hero—I felt the weight of my own journey. Like Eddy, Anthony, and Phil, I had rebuilt my life one small victory at a time. Each of these men had taught me something different about the power of incremental progress. Eddy showed me how belief fuels transformation; Anthony showed me how facing our fears one step at a time leads to breakthrough moments; and Phil proved to me that consistency and determination can overcome even life's most devastating setbacks.

Even more than that, though, these three wise men had helped me discover my true calling. I'd always known I had a gift for bringing energy and positivity to my work, but through them, I found something deeper. I wasn't just helping people recover physically. I was guiding them through the mental battle that comes with starting over, with facing seemingly impossible odds, with choosing to believe in a better future, one small victory at a time.

Looking around that media room, I realized something profound: None of these people saw me as a convicted felon because that wasn't who I was anymore. Like my clients, I had transformed myself through countless small choices, daily commitments, and incremental victories. My past hadn't disappeared, but it had become part of a larger story—one about the power of taking life one step, one choice, one victory at a time.

Throughout all this transformation, Jackie stood by me. Where Eddy showed me belief, Anthony showed me focus, and Phil showed me consistency, Jackie demonstrated unwavering loyalty. Despite my past mistakes and the ongoing challenges of my probation, she chose to build a life with me. Even when I stumbled and made the immature choice that temporarily pushed her away, she gave me another chance—recognizing the man I was becoming, not just the man I had been.

The loyalty Jackie showed wasn't blind faith. I earned her faith through my consistent actions, month after month, along with the small victories we often achieved together that built her trust in me over time. Each time I made it to work on time, each morning I helped with the kids, each restriction I navigated without complaint—these were the small wins that eventually convinced her I was worth betting on. Just as my clients had to rebuild their bodies and lives one step at a time, Jackie and I rebuilt our relationship one moment of trust at a time.

Looking back at our journey from those early days to our beach wedding and beyond, I see now that the family we created wasn't built on grand romantic gestures. It was built on thousands of small moments—driving the kids to school, showing up for work day after day, choosing to communicate rather than withdraw, practicing patience when frustrations mounted. Our relationship, like any rehabilitation process, required consistent effort, unwavering belief, focus through fears, and the loyalty to stick with it even when progress seemed slow.

Standing in the sheriff's office that day, I wasn't just a former convict sitting next to a hero. I was a man who had learned—through prison, through rehabilitation work, through marriage and fatherhood—that true transformation happens one choice, one step, one day at a time.

THE FIFTH CODE TO MIND OVER VIRTUALLY EVERYTHING:

Small wins compound into lasting change.

MOVE Sound Bite Summary

1. True progress happens through small, consistent victories—not giant leaps. Each tiny step forward creates momentum for the next one.

2. Every major transformation begins with a single action, backed by an unshakable belief in what's possible. Mental barriers often require the same incremental approach as physical ones—you conquer fear one small brave act at a time.

3. Consistency in showing up every day, even when progress feels minimal, builds the foundation for breakthrough moments.

4. Meaningful transformation happens when you stop focusing on the destination and start embracing each small step of the journey.

5. Your past does not define your future; it's the small, positive choices you make today that determine who you become tomorrow.

Chad and Jackie Dunn having fun at Tempe Town Lake,
Tempe, Arizona, October 28, 2023.

CHAPTER 6

RENT IS DUE DAILY

"Do one thing every day that scares you.
Those small things that make us uncomfortable
help us build courage to do the work we do."
—Eleanor Roosevelt

"Push through one more rep for me," I told Luis, watching him struggle through his final set of shoulder presses. During four years of training, this tough dude taught me exactly how far to challenge him. "You've got this, brother. Make it your best one."

Luis grimaced, arms trembling as he fought gravity, then locked out overhead. The weight slammed the rack with that familiar metallic clang—a sound that had echoed through my last seven years at Rehab Plus. I forced a smile, my signature energy flickering.

"Something's off with you today," Luis said, sitting up and grabbing his towel. "You're quieter than usual."

I wiped down the rack, the towel rough against my palm, buying a moment. An hour from now, I'd meet with Warren and Mitch to give them my two weeks' notice. These were the same guys who'd gambled on an ex-con, who'd transformed employers into family, and who'd stood by me when my past screamed, "Don't trust him!"

Rehab Plus had served as my proving ground. Right by the Swiss ball rack mounted to the wall, Eddy took his first steps after his spinal injury—the same place Anthony rebuilt his confidence post-burns and Phil clawed back his strength. Every inch of the space held a story of transformation, including mine. After prison, I'd pieced myself together here and discovered I could become more than my rap sheet. But it started feeling like a cage. I'd hit a ceiling—not the physical one, but the kind that signaled I had more to give, more people to help, and I couldn't accomplish it here.

I stretched Luis's back at the session's end, dodging his questions with casual conversation. When he stood up to leave, I skipped our usual fist bump and offered him a brotherly handshake with a shoulder tap.

"Everything okay, Chad?"

"Yeah, buddy," I said, forcing the upbeat tone I'd mastered. "Just feeling extra grateful today."

Quitting didn't simply mean leaving a job. It meant abandoning a sanctuary. But that voice that had pushed me to remake myself in prison was whispering to me again: Sometimes the biggest risk means playing it safe. An hour later, I sat down with Warren and Mitch, heart pounding, prepared to bet on myself all over again.

The decision to leave didn't come easily. Rehab Plus had functioned as a family, welcoming me back without hesitation after prison. I felt indebted to them. After seven years never missing a day and bringing in clients who came specifically for me, I'd repaid that debt and then some. I had a few clients I trained on my own time, but with no opportunity for advancement at my job, limited potential for increasing my income, and no avenue to pursue my vision for helping people beyond the Rehab Plus model, I made my decision. Leaving a steady salary felt like stepping off a cliff, especially as a convicted felon with few options. Companies avoid hiring guys like me; I'd discovered that when a medical equipment position vanished after a background check, despite acing the interviews.

I almost always project the most positive energy in the world, typically operating at a ten out of ten. But before resigning, that energy diminished, and Jackie noticed. Instead of bursting through the door, buzzing from a successful day, I began slumping in, dragging the weight of the day with me. The negativity I'd always brushed off started winning; Jackie didn't like seeing me that way. Then one night, I brought home a positive story, something that hadn't occurred in months.

"I've been coaching this business savant, Luis Guzman, a data scientist for PetSmart. I've never heard anyone discuss business like him. Today he told me I should launch my own venture. Crazy, huh?"

"Why does that sound crazy?"

"He just appreciates that I helped him when nobody else could. Back injuries are tricky."

Jackie leaned forward, her hands gripping her glass of iced tea, eyes steady.

"You didn't answer my question."

"Shit, you know I'd love to start my own business, but we can't afford it. Where would we find the money?"

"In the same places everyone else who starts a business finds it. Banks, for example."

She made a valid point. I knew I possessed the drive and enthusiasm to manage my own business, but the transition from salaried trainer to owner—navigating loans, licenses, risks I knew nothing about—felt overwhelming, even for my boundless optimism. I'd overcome worse odds in prison, but could I walk this tightrope without a net? In prison, I'd endured sleeping on freezing concrete floors, exploding colostomy bags, existing without freedom. But a business venture felt different. I knew the statistics: The vast majority of new businesses fail. I'd progressed so far after prison, and though I had more to contribute, I didn't know if I wanted to risk everything on those kinds of odds. But Luis had planted the seed, and Jackie provided the nourishment. The real possibility began to take root in my mind.

SEE IT AND BELIEVE IT

It only took a few days after Luis and Jackie planted the idea of establishing my own business before I dove in, clueless but determined. As part of my research and planning toward my exit, I started by contacting a commercial property owner and began searching for a location while scrambling for capital.

I approached angel investors first, thanks to my connection with Chad McKay, Mike Tyson's assistant, who introduced me to Phil Nuciola. Meeting Phil at a Life Time fitness café, notebook in hand, I felt like a gazelle facing a lion. My instincts from prison's moneyed hustlers kicked in. I requested $200,000, but his interest rate was too high. When he demanded a business plan and I fumbled my outline, he directed me to a professional. Strike one, but I'd gained knowledge: Every forward step would require I admit how much I didn't know or understand.

Next, I visited JPMorganChase bank. The loan officer smiled. "We'd love to assist you, Mr. Dunn, but we'll need a business plan."

That barrier hit me in the face again—numbers, projections, market analysis I couldn't comprehend. In prison, I'd embraced physical pain and isolation. Now my optimism strained under the burden of navigating new territory.

Eventually I told my parents about my plans, and Dad—whose own business enterprises had taught him what I didn't know yet—invited me over to their home. "Tell me about your vision," he said. I outlined my concept: a center to help anyone move, a place to break the mold. Instead of advice, he proposed giving me direct support. "Your mother and I will loan you $160,000. We'll negotiate terms." I wasn't surprised by his offer. After paying my attorney fees and court fines, they'd supported me before, but this loan represented redemption, a chance to look my dad in the eye without shame. I thanked him and gave him a big hug.

Then he challenged me: "Are you willing to sacrifice your house and relocate your family to a campground?" Failure wasn't an option, but his caution echoed his own business collapse. "I'm willing to accept that risk," I said. He nodded.

"Just understand what you're committing yourself to."

Jackie and I discovered the ideal place in Chandler, Arizona, an industrial location divided by walls that I could demolish to create an open gym layout. I saw the gym and even its name in my mind: MOVE Human Performance Center. Jackie and I contracted an architect, obtained permits, and allocated $120,000 of the $160,000 loan for renovations, gambling we'd be successful with a three-year lease.

Giving up $82,000 (a $45,000 salary from Rehab Plus and $37,000 from private clients I trained on my own) would leave us relying solely on Jackie's income. Unfortunately, renovations consumed the loan, equipment costs loomed, and suddenly, our cash flow dried up. Still, I held onto my prison-learned tenacity: Discomfort is part of the deal.

I was sticking to my timeline. It was time to notify Warren and Mitch that I'd be leaving Rehab Plus. We met at El Pollo Loco, our preferred spot, where the aroma of grilled chicken tacos and a fresh salsa bar hung heavy. This place and those smells typically comforted me, but that day they upset my stomach like prison slop. Warren leaned forward in his chair, arms folded, while Mitch munched on chips and salsa.

"Guys," I blurted out. "I'm submitting my two weeks' notice," I said, my voice cracking.

Silence. Warren's brow furrowed, his businessman's mask slipping momentarily. Then he let out a laugh. "Shit, Chadly, you're serious? You're going to be fine. Whatever you do, you'll kill it!"

Mitch put down his fork. "We'll miss you, brother."

I sighed inside with relief! They didn't fight me, didn't guilt me—just sent me off with the same trust they'd shown me seven years ago, back when I was just a number in a jumpsuit. Their faith felt like a shove forward, pushing me into the unknown I'd been dreading—and craving.

On my final day Warren and the team organized a "moving on" celebration and invited all our patients, former patients, and clients to bid me farewell. It didn't cause as much physical pain as my prison departure, but I felt just as emotional saying goodbye to all the people who had meant so much to me, and more importantly, believed in me.

WIN THE DAY

From its inception, MOVE Human Performance Center aimed to disrupt, similar to Uber and Lyft, where drivers don't require certification as cabbies, just people getting from A to B efficiently. Clients want results, not credentials, but without a physical therapist license, we couldn't process insurance claims and would build on cash payments. That motivated me to establish a facility for everyone, from spinal cord patients to stay-at-home moms, all seeking to move and move better. Naming it "MOVE" felt obvious.

I did hold certifications as a fitness trainer, a sports performance specialist, a corrective exercise specialist, and a behavioral change expert. My decade in sports medicine taught me how to develop a premier facility for injury recovery and training. We'd welcome anyone, regardless of their circumstances. In all my years working with people, I'd discovered potential in every damaged body. At MOVE, I intended to take my skills and improve the community's health with my approach. All I needed was an opportunity.

Construction exceeded our timeline by two months, but I achieved my 2,700-square-foot vision: black rubber flooring, a turf section for sprints, parallel bars for spinal clients, and equipment that included squat racks and kettlebells. We offered variety surpassing any gym I'd experienced. White walls with black and blue accents projected a modern aesthetic. The artists we commissioned painted "Mindset, Move, and Lifestyle" alongside our motto: "Mind Over Virtually Everything." I loved it! Our locker rooms featured disability-accessible showers, not for post-workout convenience, but for paralyzed clients requiring dignity after accidents. My dream materialized. Now I simply needed to populate it with life.

On May 1, 2017, Jackie and I unlocked MOVE at 7:00 a.m. I flipped on the lights and surveyed the equipment, muttering, "I have no clue what to do with this shit." Despite more than twenty years of training experience, I confronted unfamiliar tools—squat racks I'd never adjusted, parallel bars I'd only watched others use. It felt exciting but deeply uncomfortable.

Trisha Hartnett, a dedicated supporter, entered first, followed by Patty and Katie—women I'd previously trained. I projected false confidence, guiding them through new equipment fresh from the box. Internally, I scrambled, working to conceal the doubt I felt in that moment as the "confident mindset guy" and new business owner. By lunch, we'd earned $75. Jackie left for her bartending shift, and I faced an empty afternoon—no one else came. I locked up at 7:00 p.m. We'd earned $75 for twelve hours.

Driving home, I wondered if Dad was right. *Have I made a mistake?* Prison offered predictability—three square meals, a solid roof, a routine I could depend on. Launching MOVE felt like stumbling blind through the wilderness without maps or flashlights. I refused to surrender, but the stress intensified. I could lose everything, and I felt it more than ever. I finally understood why few people start businesses and why convicts return to prison.

Operating MOVE Human Performance Center helped me reverse prison's teachings. In prison, the rules, the guards, and the environment dictated my choices. At MOVE, I controlled my surroundings and made them vibrant and energized for me and our clients, but those quiet hours without clients—vacant, unsettling—mirrored the isolation I experienced in prison. Pretty soon I realized I could permit these feelings of worry and dread to destroy me or strengthen me. My fears and concerns could break me or build me. I chose to face my fears and start studying the unfamiliar equipment, dream up programs, and prepare for a bright future for myself, my family, and our clients. I spent time with Jackie playing lawn darts; her laughter and her belief in me became my lifeline against the void.

MOVE's initial schedule demanded constant effort—early mornings, extended days, private clients across the city. I worked sixty-plus hours a week, opening at 5:00 a.m. for Luis, closing late for the after-work crew. Eddy, Anthony, and high school athletes joined us. By month's end, we hit thirty-five sessions, grossing $2,650—barely covering rent after costs. Numbers grew, but sustainability felt distant. We needed more buzz.

On June 3, 2017, we hosted a grand opening for MOVE, previously delayed by permit issues but featuring bike ramps, Stuntmasters, and Sunfare foods. My BMX background and Eddy's inspiration fueled the event. We took time to acknowledge the dedication that brought us here. A hundred attendees participated, and social media circulated videos, though the impact remained uncertain. Still, it juiced Jackie and I to keep pushing, a symbolic victory after months of hard work.

Mondays and Wednesdays remained largely unbooked, so I hit the streets, targeting the Islands Community with five hundred, quickly printed fliers. This time, rather than drugs, I peddled health by giving brief, sincere pitches to anyone who'd listen. After two days, this grassroots marketing approach yielded results and attracted new clients. That personal connection awakened me to networking's effectiveness. Social media posts paled in comparison to genuine human interactions.

I started to work with Art Dye, my "one in a row" mentor, helping his basketball athletes every Sunday at the Boys & Girls Club in Guadalupe. I'd have loved a break (sixty-five-hour weeks were brutal), but Art's referrals brought high school clients to MOVE. Another win, but we needed more clients to survive.

The rest of 2017 we grinded. With our heads down, clients trickled in. By November, we hit eighty sessions weekly, nearly quadrupling our start. By summer 2018, more than a hundred sessions. Still, losses mounted. In 2017, we lost $21,000; in 2018, $22,000. Debt hit $50,000, interest piling. Each month became more uncomfortable. Jackie joined MOVE full-time, trading bartending for admin and training. Her income vanished, but she picked up bartending at event gigs—never enough to replace her wage, but every dollar helped keep us afloat. We both knew something had to change or our dream would end.

Dad's warning ("You better be willing to lose your home") grew louder as MOVE teetered, debt mounting, each month more difficult. I stayed positive, worked harder, but grit alone wouldn't fix it. In August 2018, Jackie cut through my optimism.

In the empty gym at MOVE one morning, she said, emotionless, "Chad, we have to sell the house or close MOVE." I knew her math was right. She'd poured her soul into our home, every paint stroke, fixture, and design choice a piece of her dream.

"My parents' rental," I started.

"Already talked to them about it," she cut in. "It's small, old, but we'll handle it. The savings will keep MOVE alive another year."

The rental was a step down, a far cry from our remodeled home, but better than a campground. The house sold within a week. Watching Jackie touch our home's walls one last time, I saw her resolve, her sacrifice for my dream. "Ready?" she asked, eyes clear and determined. I nodded; we'd face it together, one day at a time.

After moving into the rental, Dad said, "Congrats on making it to year two in your business. I'm proud, but it sounds like you bought a job." He meant a business should run without me, freeing time for family. I loved helping clients, but he was right. I needed to build a company, not just survive the grind.

BEGINNINGS OF A COMPANY

The initial quarter of 2019 mirrored the conclusion of 2018. We continued operations but recognized we needed substantial changes to ensure long-term viability. Our primary deficiency: a licensed physical therapist. I'd recognized this limitation from the beginning and thought I could overcome it, but as client numbers grew, I realized MOVE required the physical therapy component. Without completing my education or obtaining licensure, we couldn't bill insurance for treatments. Though I could assist PT clients extensively, most relied on insurance coverage to offset costs, leaving substantial potential revenue untapped.

In April 2019 Jackie and I advertised for a physical therapist. Our challenge: We couldn't provide the $85,000 salary other facilities offered. We needed creative solutions to attract an ambitious physical therapist. Our plan involved bringing someone on board as a partner who could use their own business identity and operate within our facility. This arrangement would give them immediate access to our established client base, plus every prospective patient who entered our doors. As additional incentive, we offered them 70 percent of the profit from each client.

This arrangement lacked traditional employment security but offered an ambitious practitioner potentially higher earnings than standard PT positions. It created mutual discomfort: Our new hire surrendered conventional job security while we shared control of our space and reputation. But I'd learned that the most meaningful partnerships often start with both sides being a little uncomfortable. That's how you know you're building something different. It didn't take long to fill the spot. A young physical therapist named Crystal Masnec took the job. I'd met her when she interned at Rehab Plus. She was a perfect fit.

Crystal established her physical therapy practice called XERT Physical Therapy within MOVE Human Performance Center. Our client base expanded rapidly from two sessions the initial week to twenty-three by her fourth week in April 2019. By August, we averaged forty sessions weekly. MOVE's direct profit from the arrangement remained modest, but that additional 30 percent significantly reduced our operating deficit. Despite early success, by year's end, Crystal preferred to transition from partner to employee. We generated good income, but treating clients while also trying to run her own business was grinding her down.

Though unexpected, this shift created an ideal opportunity since MOVE had already handled insurance billing for her services, allowing us to officially market ourselves as a licensed physical therapy provider accepting insurance. We formed a new S corporation, branded as MOVE Human Performance Center and Physical Therapy, and honored Crystal's request to become an employee. The change worked in our favor and ultimately saved the business. It was the breakthrough we needed. All it took to get there was refusing to quit and embracing some uncomfortable changes.

Despite all the hurdles, we'd survived our first three years in business. Things were finally looking good for us. Crystal's addition had transformed MOVE from surviving to thriving. The gym was consistently full of high energy. Every week new clients walked through our doors, many saying they'd heard about us through word of mouth. We weren't just a gym anymore. We were becoming known as the place that could handle the tough cases, the ones other facilities turned away.

But just as we started to feel comfortable, the world had other plans. I always say the only things that can stop you are faith and nature. Then nature kicked in the door with COVID-19. I felt the floor crack beneath everything we'd bled for.

THE SIXTH CODE TO MIND OVER VIRTUALLY EVERYTHING:

Get comfortable being uncomfortable.

MOVE Sound Bite Summary

1. Growth occurs when you venture beyond familiar territory. Consistently choosing safety guarantees stagnation.

2. Authentic confidence doesn't mean knowing everything. It means feeling secure enough to keep learning and growing.

3. Personal transformation demands calculated risks and self-belief, even amid uncertainty about outcomes.

4. Achieving success frequently necessitates making others uneasy with your decisions.

5. Creating new solutions means being willing to let go of what's familiar and comfortable.

CHAPTER 7

ON THE OTHER SIDE OF PAIN

"The wound is the place where light enters you."
—Rumi

In early March 2020, I pushed through the glass doors of a medical plaza near MOVE, the faint hum of fluorescent lights buzzing overhead. My arms cradled a stack of prescription pads and business cards—hard-earned tokens of a dream that had taken three years to build. We'd clawed our way up from nothing, selling our house to keep the lights on, and now, with Crystal handling physical therapy, Jackie steering operations, and Kaine anchoring training, I could finally focus on growth. The air smelled faintly of antiseptic as I stepped into an urgent care, ready to pitch our services. But something felt off.

The waiting room was eerily silent—no coughing patients, no rustling magazines—just a receptionist perched behind a fresh sheet of plexiglass that hadn't existed the week before. Her eyes flicked up, wary as I approached. In the back, staff huddled near a coffee machine, their voices low but sharp-edged. "Pandemic," I heard someone say, the word hanging like smoke. "They're saying it's bad." I stood there, waiting to see a doctor, feeling the first ripple of something I couldn't name.

When I finally got in, the doctor barely glanced at my materials. Charts and sanitizer bottles cluttered his desk. "It's going to be interesting with this pandemic," he said, shaking his head. "Everything's about to change." I nodded politely, but his words slid off me. I'd navigated darker storms—years in the criminal underworld, two years pacing a federal prison yard. A virus? It didn't register on my radar. I thanked him, grabbed my stack, and moved to the next office. There, the tension thickened. A doctor barked orders to his staff, prepping for a shutdown.

"We have to protect ourselves," he said, his voice clipped. "We don't know what's coming." That's when it clicked. Fear had already outpaced any virus, spreading like wildfire through whispers and widened eyes. I'd seen it before in prison: Rumors of a lockdown could unravel a yard faster than any real threat. Fear made people freeze or flail—both dead ends. I refused to let it steer me.

Back at MOVE, the late afternoon sun slanted through our windows, casting long shadows across the turf. My stack of marketing materials barely had a dent in it. Every doctor seemed too busy battening down their own hatches to talk business. Jackie stood at the front desk, her phone glowing in her hands, her usual steadiness replaced by a rare intensity.

"They're talking about shutting everything down," she said, not looking up. "All nonessential businesses."

I thought of the sweat and sacrifice we'd poured into this place—the late nights, the setbacks, the momentum we'd finally built. "We're not shutting down," I said, my voice steady. She lifted her eyes and smiled, a spark of defiance mirroring mine. "I know."

In prison, I'd learned a hard truth: Fear cripples more than anything. I'd watched men crumble under rumors, lose themselves to what might happen. With MOVE on the line, I saw the same pattern unfolding—only this time, I had a choice. While others braced to hide, we'd brace to fight. As the storm approached, we were determined to ride it out and survive.

ADAPT OR DIE

The next two weeks hit like a hurricane. Local and national government mandates flew in each morning presenting a fresh tangle of rules about which businesses could survive. Business owners like us were scrambling to understand how to operate under constantly shifting conditions. Regulations changed hourly, requiring continuous adaptation of our business model. The CDC implemented six-foot social distancing requirements, then Governor Doug Ducey ended the statewide lockdown on May 15, 2020, while Maricopa County simultaneously mandated facial coverings. All these regulations were supposedly designed to help businesses—large or small—to survive but navigating them was like trying to hit a moving target in the dark.

Phoenix slowed to a ghostly hush outside our gym's windows, streets emptying as fear tightened its grip. But inside MOVE, we drew a line. Jackie's words echoed in my head: "If they want us closed, they'll have to drag us out."

The same night Governor Ducey locked down the state Jackie and I sat in the dim glow of the gym after closing, the hum of the air conditioner filling the silence. "We need a plan," she said.

"Something to show we mean business, even if the virus doesn't scare us."

I nodded.

A client from a company called TGen, a cancer research lab, mentioned high heat might kill the virus. The next day, another client—a gruff construction guy—dropped off an industrial steamer he'd snagged for a curtain job. "Use it," he grunted, and we did. Every night, we'd roll that beast across the facility, steam curling up from handles, the air thick with heat and purpose.

We went further. A thermal camera mounted at the entrance snapped photos and flagged fevers. We spaced out sessions, shrank group sizes, turned chaos into rhythm. But Crystal provided the real lifeline. As our licensed physical therapist, we could classify MOVE as an essential medical facility and keep helping people who needed it. She documented every session, her notes a shield against any audit.

Out on the streets, runners and cyclists weaved through the stillness. This new restricted environment reminded me of my time in holding facilities—guys rigging weights from trash bags and doing burpees in their cells. Humans need to move; our design demands it. We centered on giving our clients a safe harbor for moving and created a structure for doing it. Volleyball players, basketball kids, football crews—each group had their space and time. Crystal's presence allowed us to continue treating patients in need of rehabilitation, which enabled us to keep training athletes. Suddenly, MOVE transformed from a gym into a sanctuary.

A pack of elite girl gymnasts, ages twelve to thirteen with college dreams, rolled in because their regular spot had been shuttered. "Bring your gear," I told their moms. We laid out the air tumbling tracks and mats, their flips slicing the air while others Zoomed cartwheels in living rooms. Word spread. College athletes followed, then poured in a seven-foot-two Maryland center, a GCU soccer player, half of Oregon's football team.

BREAKING BARRIERS THROUGH COMMUNITY

The gym's air buzzed with sweat and determination as MOVE evolved beyond a refuge into a proving ground. Out there, the world hid behind locked doors, but inside our walls, people fought back. Not just against a virus, but against the limits it tried to impose. I'd learned in prison that those who thrived didn't wait for the storm to pass—they danced in it. Now I watched that truth unfold in real time seeing our clients' faces and stories transform their pain into extraordinary strength and resilience.

Amid these battles, a quieter crisis brewed. High school seniors faced a 2020 without graduations, their caps and gowns never to be thrown in celebration. One morning, watching our young athletes slump with the news, I turned to Jackie. "Let's host it here. We qualify as essential; we've got space." She lit up, rallying everyone—DTG Tacos catered, and Eddy King pedaled in to give the commencement speech from an exercise bike, his paralysis-defying story lifting the spirits of everyone in the room. Twenty kids got the graduation celebration they'd earned. Caps flew, families wept, toilet paper zeros on our "2020" shirts—a cheeky nod to the COVID toilet paper hoarding madness. This ceremony represented more than a milestone; it symbolized our stand. While the world shrank, we expanded—together.

A year into the pandemic with MOVE still standing, Krysten Muir limped through our doors in May 2021, her unstable body bracing a walker while scraping the turf's edge. A car accident had shattered her back, leaving her paralyzed at twenty-one—the first girl to kick a field goal in AIA high school football history was now fighting to stand again. A local reporter, Cam Cox, had connected us after covering Eddy King's spinal cord recovery. "She feels isolated," he'd said. "She's in the hospital, but COVID keeps her family out." I understood that loneliness—it gnaws worse than any injury. I messaged her on Instagram: "I've walked this road with others. We'll get through it together." Her reply came as a groggy voice note: "Can't type, too doped up. I just want my family." My gut twisted. This involved more than legs. Her spirit needed help.

Doctors preached caution. "Manage expectations," they said. But I saw the same fire in Krysten that I'd seen in Eddy King. It's the kind that turns "impossible" into a dare. "We're not just getting you walking," I told her on day one. "We're getting you to kick a field goal again." She stared at me like I'd lost it. We started small having her crawl like an infant. We worked with her to wake up her nerves with electric pulses and balance on shaky ground. "Pain signals weakness leaving the body," I'd say. Krysten would grit her teeth and push harder. Some days the hurt won, and doubt clawed at her. On those days, tears would streak down her face, but she kept showing up.

Krysten's breakthrough happened months later when she was standing alone with no walker. People's chatter in the gym faded as their heads turned. Then came Krysten's first steps—slow and trembling, but hers. At that point, we rigged a push sled, the turf crunching under it as she pushed, reconnecting her spirit to the athlete she'd been. Patients paused their reps to clap; high school kids shouted encouragement. A year and a half after the crash, January 2022, Krysten stood on a football field with news cameras rolling. It was time for her to kick that field goal we talked about eighteen months earlier. The ball sailed through the uprights, a clean arc against the sky. The people there supporting Krysten roared. In that moment, she didn't just reclaim her legs; she reclaimed herself.

Krysten's triumph was a powerful testament to the resilience that MOVE nurtures, but her story was just one of many that defined our community's spirit. Rewind to June 2021, when Carrick Felix, a six-foot-five NBA veteran I'd rehabbed years earlier at Rehab Plus, reached out with a bold challenge that embodied the same grit Krysten displayed. "Chad, I've got this crazy idea," his voice crackled through my phone. He wanted to run thirty-one miles on his thirty-first birthday in August, facing Arizona's brutal heat head-on. Like Krysten, Carrick's journey was about more than physical endurance. It showcased the unyielding determination and community support that MOVE champions, pushing each member to redefine their limits.

"A marathon's 26.2 miles," I reminded him. "You're adding five miles onto that with the heat, ya know."

Carrick laughed. "Go big or go home," he said.

We had the tools—turf, cryo chamber, mindset. He even trained beside Krysten some days, her resolve fueling his. The day arrived, and his 5:00 a.m. start time flopped because his team overslept. Most would've quit. Not Carrick. At 1:00 p.m., heat shimmering off the asphalt, he took off alone from Bartlett Lake. I found him later near McDowell Road, rain streaking his face, legs screaming but moving. I rolled beside him, camera out, yelling, "Ah! Let's go! Let's go, baby!"

From the start of the run, it was twenty-nine miles and seven-and-a-half hours later when Carrick was crossing the Tempe Town Lake bridge. Lights flared as Carrick crossed Tempe Town Lake and passed the ASU sign: "Making a Better Place Because of You." Then at 8:58 p.m., he sprinted the last four hundred yards to the Desert Financial Arena to finish at 9:00 p.m. Champagne sprayed as we celebrated together. Thirty-one miles, no excuses. That's MOVE—embracing the hard road, not the easy out.

These victories didn't stand in isolation. They provided proof—pain bends you, but community breaks you through.

Krysten kicked, Carrick ran, and 2020 grads celebrated, not alone, but with the MOVE community behind them. That momentum carried us all forward, past survival into achieving even more than we had dreamed was possible.

GROWTH AND PURPOSE

By early 2022 MOVE was bursting at the seams. Seven-foot basketball players ducked under doorframes, rehab patients maneuvered past turf drills, and collegiate athletes jostled for space, all in our 2,700-square-foot facility. The air pulsed with effort, but the walls were closing in with our limited space. One day, the landlord tossed out a lifeline: "The suite next door's available."

Jackie's eyes lit up, her mind already racing. "We could double down," she said, tracing blueprints in the air. The world still reeled from the pandemic, uncertainty thick as desert dust, but I heard my dad's voice from years back when MOVE existed only as a spark: "Son, you gotta spend money to make money—just spend it right." This felt right.

With timing in our favor, we jumped on it. I traveled with the AZ Compass Prep basketball squad sweating through their Florida GEICO High School Nationals Tournament while Jackie turned chaos into progress back home. She wrangled permits, sketched layouts, and barked at contractors, her voice cutting through the whine of saws. One afternoon, they punched through the wall between suites—a jagged hole spilling in light and possibility. Dust swirled as we added 2,100 square feet, bringing us to 5,455. We didn't miss a beat. Clients trained on one side, hammers pounded on the other, the rhythm of growth syncing with our pulse.

We had rolled out more turf for agility, lined up a full dumbbell rack gleaming under the lights, and carved niches for rehab and performance. The crown jewel? A cryotherapy chamber humming at negative 127 degrees. Its icy mist promised optimal recovery. I'd tell clients, "Your body reacts the same to hot and cold stress situations."

With cryotherapy, we're trying to drop your core temperature by 40 to 50 percent, down to around fifty degrees. We typically place people in the chamber for six minutes to achieve this temperature drop, which causes blood vessels to constrict, decreasing swelling and triggering an increased release of endorphins that reduce pain. Essentially, your brain helps your body survive a stressful activity, like in prison. The human body reacts to both hot and cold stress the same way. Every other type of stress is relative or mental. Now we could take someone from injury to peak in one unbroken arc: MOVE's PT crew mending them, cryo healing them, our turf pushing them past their old limits. We'd evolved beyond a gym into a machine for transformation.

The team grew as our space expanded. Kaine, who'd started as an ASU intern logging 270 hours, became my shadow. He was a basketball-obsessed, relentless kid who saw MOVE's soul the way I did. When COVID axed other internships, we kept ours alive, and that's how Brandon Blair walked in. An A.T. Still University PT intern under Crystal, Brandon bridged rehab and grit like he'd been born for it. After passing his boards, we locked him in full-time, his quiet focus perfectly complementing Kaine's fire. Austin Carr joined too. He was another PT with steady hands and a hunger to tackle the tough cases. Each new hire contributed something—gears firing in perfect unison inside the engine we built.

Crystal eventually left us to pursue virtual PT, but by then, we stood solid. Brandon stepped up as director of physical therapy. His philosophy mirrored ours: Treat the person, not the problem. Then Kaine took a Compass kid through drills on the same turf, sweat flying, while Austin guided a post-op warrior nearby. Orchestrated chaos reigned at MOVE, but the chaos was the beautiful kind. Every square foot of our facility felt alive with purpose.

Looking back, expanding mid-pandemic sounds nuts; it was like jumping off a cliff with no net. But staying small would've choked us. My prison days taught me stagnation kills faster than risk. When Jackie and I weighed the pros and cons and sold our house to save MOVE, that decision became a gamble that paid off. Now every lesson we'd learned was clicking into place. We hadn't been reckless. We had taken calculated risks and bet on ourselves and on the community we'd forged.

That first growth period hurt—money stretched thin, sleepless nights, doubts gnawing. But my dad's experience and wisdom spoke truth to me: Spend it right, and it multiplies. The new space let us breathe, serve, and innovate. A pro athlete could grind beside someone relearning to walk, their stories crossing in the air. High school kids saw resilience in rehab patients, fuel for their own dreams. We'd built a circle, and it spun faster with every life we touched.

This success transcended mere survival. It was evolution. The struggles, the gambles, the walls we broke through—they sharpened us. Every crack in our past had let light in, and that light was blinding. We hadn't finished growing—not by a long shot—but we'd found our *why*: to push people past their breaking points, together, into something greater.

LIGHT THROUGH THE CRACKS

Pain's a brutal teacher, but it's better than any other instructor I've had. In prison, pain stripped me bare. It showed me that resilience forms in fire. On the streets, it nearly broke me, until I clawed back through the hell of recovery. Building MOVE, every setback, from selling our house to facing a pandemic, carved a path to a bigger future we hadn't even imagined.

The pandemic could've ended us. Instead, we adapted. We steamed the gym, found a way to qualify as essential, and threw open our doors when others shut theirs. Adversity didn't dictate our choices; it drove us to innovate. Krysten Muir kicked a field goal from a wheelchair's ashes because we built structure. Carrick Felix ran thirty-one miles in blistering heat, not because it came easy, but because our community pushed him past his mind's quit. AZ Compass kids helped turn our turf into an NBA pipeline, proving resilience amplifies when we grind together.

That cryotherapy chamber, humming at negative 127, sums this lesson up: Growth lives at discomfort's edge. Step in, shiver, emerge stronger. The body heals where the mind dares to go. Every client, from our rehab patients to our pros, walked that line with us. We expanded mid-storm, broke walls, bet on people—Kaine's fire, Brandon's steady hands, Jackie's steel—because the best investments don't play safe; they move boldly.

THE SEVENTH CODE TO MIND OVER VIRTUALLY EVERYTHING:

On the other side of pain awaits greatness.

MOVE Sound Bite Summary

1. Don't let fear paralyze you; use it to ignite new paths and outmaneuver the storm.

2. Build a framework that bends, not breaks, so you can move when the world locks down.

3. Push your mind past the pain, and your body will follow. No will, no way.

4. Lean on others who fight the same battles; together, you'll outlast anything solo.

5. Step into the sting, the cold, the hard shit. That's where you'll discover what you're made of.

CHAPTER 8

MAKE THE DIFFERENCE

"Your past mistakes don't determine your future success."
—Zig Ziglar

For years I carried my past like a concrete block strapped to my back, terrified it'd crush everything I'd built: my training facility, MOVE, my reputation as a trainer, the trust of the parents who sent their kids to me, the elite athletes who flew in from across the country to work with me.

I'd spent over a decade editing my story down to a safe, sanitized version of Chad Dunn: the kid who raced BMX, wrestled in high school, started as a jack of all trades at Rehab Plus, and eventually built a gym where the impossible became possible—where paralyzed athletes learned to move again, where high school kids trained alongside pros. It was a good story. A clean story. But it wasn't a true story.

I left out the darker chapters: the drug dealing that started small and spiraled out of control, the drug use that numbed me to the wreckage I caused, the two years in federal prison where I hit rock bottom, the shame that clung to me like a shadow even after I'd walked free. Hiding those chapters of my life exhausted me, like running a marathon with weights chained to my ankles. I thought I had to protect what Jackie and I had built, until one tense afternoon in the gym cracked that belief wide open and showed me my past might serve as the key to saving others.

THE SPARK: A STANDOFF IN THE GYM

The air during the AZ Compass Prep workout hung thick with tension that day, like a storm brewing before the first lightning strike. Two of my basketball players—one older, a senior with a chip on his shoulder and scouts already circling him; the other younger, a sophomore still finding his place—stood chest-to-chest over something as trivial as a pair of headphones. The younger player had asked his teammate to take them off during our workout, following my rule about staying focused: no distractions, no excuses. The older player refused.

"Don't be telling me what to do," he snapped, stepping closer, his fists balled at his sides, the veins in his forearms popping like he was prepared to swing.

The younger player didn't back down, his jaw tight, eyes narrowing as he squared up. I could see it escalating in slow motion—the way their shoulders tensed, the way the other players stopped their dynamic warm-up drills to watch, the way the air seemed to buzz with the unspoken threat of violence.

Their coach tried to step in, his voice rising as he attempted to defuse the situation. "Come on, man. We're a team. We're a team."

But his words might as well have been a whisper against a hurricane. They bounced off the gym walls, unheard, as the standoff stretched through the workout, threatening to boil over at any second.

These weren't just any players. They belonged to our elite AZ Compass Prep program. Both players had Division I offers piling up and potential NBA futures glimmering on the horizon if they didn't sabotage themselves first. Many of these players came from backgrounds I knew too well: single-parent homes where moms or dads worked double shifts, neighborhoods where respect functioned as currency that you earned with your fists or lost it with your fear. I spent years in those same streets—South Phoenix, Guadalupe— where every corner held a story, and not all of them had happy endings. I understood their world better than they realized, better than I'd ever let on. But watching those two players that day, their pride and anger locking them into a collision course, I saw myself at their age: quick to fight, slow to think, one bad choice away from a path I couldn't walk back from.

After the drills, with the tension still hanging heavy, I called the team over. "Sit down for a second," I said, my voice steady but firm. "I want to put something in perspective."

They slumped onto the turf right next to our cryotherapy chamber, the older player crossing his arms tight across his chest, the younger one staring at the floor, his knee bouncing with unspent energy. The rest of the team shuffled in around them, curious but wary. I'd kept my past locked away in a vault for years, trying to protect MOVE, protect my reputation, and protect the fragile trust I'd built with our clients and their families. Jackie and I had poured everything into MOVE. We'd sold our house to keep the doors open during COVID. We'd also worked eighteen-hour days to make our place a sanctuary where elite athletes trained alongside people relearning to walk after spinal injuries. The last thing I wanted was for my past to undo all that. But standing there, looking at these young men—kids who reminded me so much of my younger self, kids one wrong turn from the mistakes I'd made—I felt something shift deep in my gut. Maybe hiding my story wasn't protecting anyone. Maybe it was holding me back from the kind of impact I needed to make.

"We're a team here," I started, my voice quieter now, forcing them to lean in to hear me. "You can't put yourself on a pedestal above each other. When I was in prison . . ." I paused, letting the words hang in the air like a grenade with the pin pulled. Their eyes widened, heads snapping up from their phones and the floor. This wasn't the script they expected from their trainer, the guy who worked with NBA prospects. I could see the questions flickering in their faces: Prison? For real? What the hell?

"When I was in prison," I continued, "if I acted like a jackass or wanted to fight somebody over something stupid, I put myself out there alone. In prison, you don't survive alone. You need your brothers. I had guys who had my back because we functioned as a team. We went to war for and with each other. But more importantly, we kept each other out of trouble. That defines a team, which doesn't mean being the toughest guys in the room. It means having each other's backs, keeping each other straight."

The gym fell silent. The hostility that had simmered all session seemed to evaporate, replaced by something new—attention, respect, curiosity. The two players who were ready to throw punches exchanged a look, the older one giving a slight nod to the younger, a silent truce. The rest of the team shifted in their seats, some leaning forward, others staring at me like they saw me for the first time.

Driving home that night, my hands felt loose on the wheel, like I'd dropped a fifty-pound weight I didn't even know I'd been carrying. The city lights blurred past me, and for the first time in years, I didn't feel the familiar knot of dread in my chest when I was afraid that someone would find out, that my past would unravel everything Jackie and I had built. Instead, I kept seeing their faces in my mind—those wide-eyed looks of respect, the way the tension had melted into something like understanding. I'd shared a piece of my truth, unfiltered, and it hadn't destroyed anything. It had built something instead. Watching those young men transform from potential enemies to teammates through the power of my story, I realized something profound: My past wasn't a burden I had to overcome; it was a tool I could use to help others overcome theirs. I just didn't know how to take that next step—or if I was even ready to.

THE WEIGHT OF HIDING

That moment with the basketball players cracked something open in me. But it also forced me to confront the weight I'd carried for years. Hiding my truth didn't represent just a choice; it demanded a daily grind, a constant mental battle of what to say, what to leave out, who we could trust and with how much. At MOVE, I'd constructed a careful divide between who I was now and who I'd been back then. My clients knew me as the trainer who worked with elite athletes, the guy who could push them through their physical and mental barriers to hit new personal records or walk again after a spinal injury. They saw the Chad Dunn who'd built a gym where NBA prospects sweated alongside grandmothers relearning to climb stairs, where high school kids dreamed big while watching burn victims fight for every inch of mobility.

But they didn't know about the barriers I'd pushed through myself—drug dealing that started as a hustle and ended in handcuffs, drug use that turned me into someone I didn't recognize, two years in federal prison where I stared down the wreckage of my choices. Even Art Dye, my mentor and friend for over a decade, didn't know my full story. He saw me as the guy who understood "one in a row," helping athletes build success one small victory at a time. He didn't know I'd used that same principle to claw my way out of prison, putting my life back together one day at a time.

Jackie had always fiercely protected our business, and I couldn't blame her. "People judge quickly," she'd say whenever the subject came up. "They don't see who you are now. They just see what they want to see."

She spoke truth. I'd lived it. Years ago, when I worked at Rehab Plus, a colleague's wife had pulled her young daughter away from me one day. "Don't go over there," she'd whispered loud enough for me to hear. "He's a bad guy." I'd just started rebuilding my life then, fresh out of prison, trying to prove myself beyond my mistakes. But to her, I embodied a cautionary tale she didn't want her kid near me. That moment seared itself into me—a lesson to keep my past buried deep, to never let it slip out where someone could weaponize it against me. This strategy worked for a while, but the cost was steep. Every time I dodged a question about my background, every time I bit my tongue when a client thanked me for understanding their struggles, it felt like swallowing glass. I operated at half-power, giving them part of me but never the whole.

Each morning at MOVE I'd walk past the words painted on our wall: "Mind Over Virtually Everything." This message represented more than a slogan. It told how I'd survived, how I'd rebuilt my life, how I pushed my clients to keep going when they wanted to quit. It turned out that hiding part of myself created its own kind of prison, one I'd built brick by brick with every half-truth and sidestepped question. That moment with the basketball players had shown me my past could serve as a tool if I had the courage to use it. But bravery wasn't enough on its own. I needed an opportunity, a push, something to tip me over the edge from hiding to sharing. What I didn't know was that breakthrough would come through an old friend fighting his own battles. He was someone who'd known me before the fall, stuck with me through the rise, and would soon challenge me to stop running from the truth.

THE TURNING POINT: BRANDAN'S PODCAST

In June 2021, Brandan Millan walked through MOVE's doors with a knee injury he was hell-bent on fixing without surgery. We went all the way back to elementary school where we'd once gotten into a fistfight over some kid stuff neither of us could even remember now. Most likely it was who was the badass in our apartment complex as we played on the giant concrete tubes in the playground area. King of the tubes led to name-calling, which led to a fight! Life took us in different directions after high school. He went on to play college ball and wrestle in California. Then he carved out a solid path as a fire captain, custom home builder, and family man.

Seeing Brandan walk into MOVE after all those years felt like a time warp. He still possessed that same intensity, that warrior spirit. The kind of guy who'd ride up South Mountain on a single-speed bike, while others coasted on electric ones, sweat pouring off him but a grin on his face like he dared the hill to break him. Now, though, he carried a new weight in his eyes. His mother had just passed, and he'd set his sights on winning a World IBJJF Championship in jiujitsu's Master Blue Belt division. He didn't want to win just for the title but as a tribute to her memory. When he asked me to help with his training, I understood immediately. Sometimes the physical challenge functions as a vehicle for something deeper, a way to honor what you've lost by proving what you still can accomplish.

Working alongside his coach at Team Carlson Gracie, we focused on efficiency of movement. At our age—pushing fifty, with more scars than we'd like to admit—you can't just power through everything like you did at twenty. You have to strategize more intelligently. "Efficiency matters most," Brandan would say, his voice steady as he adjusted his stance on the mat, sweat beading on his forehead. Between his firefighting shifts, his construction projects, and his training, every minute had to count. I threw myself into his prep like it was my fight. I designed mobility drills to loosen up his hips, prescribed strength exercises to stabilize his knee, and tweaked his conditioning to maximize endurance without risking injury. Four weeks into our work together, he won the Pan Am Games. With a gold medal hanging around his neck, he grinned through the pain, soaking wet, but Brandan's spirit was untouchable. The preparation paid off, just as we knew it would.

Then Brandan pursued another goal I didn't see coming, one that would hit me harder than any takedown on the mat. He hosted a podcast called *Make the Difference*, where he interviewed people about how they'd impacted others' lives. Guests included firefighters who'd pulled families from burning buildings, coaches who'd turned kids' futures around, and everyday folks who'd accomplished extraordinary things. One day in early September, after a particularly grueling session where we'd pushed each other to the brink, he turned to me. The gym was quiet except for the hum of the AC. "Chad," he said, his tone shifting to serious now, "I want you to come on the podcast. Tell your story."

The words landed like a sucker punch. My immediate instinct was to deflect, to protect the carefully constructed image I'd built for myself over the years. I laughed it off, muttering something about not having much to say, but inside, my mind raced. Tell my story? The real one? The one I'd buried so deep I sometimes forgot where I'd left the shovel? I thought about MOVE. I thought about the parents who trusted me with their kids and the sponsors who invested in our programs. I thought about clients like Eddy and Krysten whose recoveries had made the news. What if they heard about my past and walked away? What if they saw me as that "bad guy" from Rehab Plus all over again? Despite my objections, Brandan wouldn't back off. "You've got something people need to hear," he said. "Not the shiny stuff—the real shit."

I told him I'd think about it, but truthfully, I couldn't stop thinking about it. That night, I sat in my Tahoe outside our house, the engine off, the streetlight casting long shadows across the dashboard. I weighed the risks. If I did this, there'd be no going back. Someone—maybe a client, maybe a parent, maybe a competitor—could hear it and decide I wasn't worthy of trust. MOVE could take a massive hit. Jackie could get hurt by the fallout. Then I thought about the basketball players who'd listened when I'd let just a piece of my truth slip out. What if Brandan was right? What if my story—the messy, ugly, real one—could do more than I'd ever done by hiding it?

I talked it over with Jackie later that night, pacing our living room while she sat on the couch, her arms crossed, listening with that quiet intensity she always brought when the stakes were high. To my surprise, she didn't shut it down. "You can do the podcast," she said, her voice measured but firm, "but you can't mention MOVE. Don't tie it to the business at all." I understood her concern. Kids trained here, parents trusted us with their futures, and one wrong move could unravel years of work. "If someone finds the podcast and listens to it, that's fine," she said. "But we don't promote it through MOVE's channels. Deal?" I agreed.

The day of the recording, I drove to Brandan's construction office in Tempe, a squat brick building off the 101. He'd set up a small sound room in the back—a makeshift studio, two mics on a wooden desk, and a couple of professional studio chairs. His friend Kirk, a fellow firefighter who helped with the podcast, ran the soundboard. Chris, one of Brandan's friends, cohosted. I felt my palms sweat as I sat down. The mic stared at me like a judge waiting for a confession. Brandan sensed my anxiety as he adjusted his headset, his voice calm but direct. "Just talk," he said, giving me a nod. "Tell your story like you're telling it to me. Forget about everyone else who might listen."

For two hours in that special room, with the soft whirring of the recording equipment amplifying every breath, I let the walls come down. Brandan and Chris didn't just interview me. They guided me through my own story, helping me connect dots I hadn't even realized existed there. We talked about the drug dealing—how it started as a way to make quick cash in my early twenties, but snowballed into something I couldn't control, with deals going bad and debts piling up. We talked about the drug use—how I'd started using to escape the stress, the guilt, the voice in my head telling me I screwed up my life, until I sank so deep, I barely recognized myself in the mirror. We talked about prison—the arrest that came like a thunderclap, the two years inside prison, the nights I'd lie awake on a thin mattress, staring at the concrete ceiling, replaying every choice that had landed me there. But we also talked about transformation—all the choices I made in prison to better myself; how I'd promised myself to come out better, not bitter; how I'd channeled that same reckless energy that got me locked up into building MOVE and into helping others rebuild their own lives.

The words flowed easier than I'd expected, like water breaking through a dam I'd held back for too long. By the time we wrapped, I felt raw, exposed, like I'd been strip-searched again, hiding nothing. Kirk, who'd worked the sound, took off his headphones and shook his head, his voice low. "Man," he said, "people need to hear this." I wasn't so sure. On the drive home, doubt crept in like a fog. Had I said too much? Would people look at me differently now? Would they see the man I'd become, or just the felon I'd been?

When I told Jackie I'd finished the recording, she asked to listen to it before we shared it with anyone else. I sat on the edge of our couch as she connected to the Bluetooth speaker, pressed play, and began to clean the house while she listened. Two hours later, she looked at me, not with worry or concern, but with pride. "This is badass." We decided to share it carefully at first, sending the link to a few trusted clients—all adults—to gauge their reactions.

The responses started coming in almost immediately, and they weren't what I'd braced for. One client, a single dad who'd brought his son to MOVE for football training, texted me: "I never knew . . . this explains so much about why you excel at what you do. Respect."

A mother from a family we know well called to say she cried listening to it, not out of judgment but because it made her understand her own struggles with addiction in a new light.

Another client, a mom whose daughter trained with us, asked if her teenage son could listen too. "He's getting into trouble, and I think this might help him see a way out."

More surprising than all this positive feedback was the complete absence of negative reactions. Not a single client pulled away. No parents withdrew their kids from training. Instead, people listened, they trusted us more. The story they'd heard didn't make them question what I did. It made them value why I did it.

Even Jackie's perspective shifted after seeing those responses. One night, as we closed up MOVE, the gym was silent except for the faint clink of weights settling on racks. That's when she turned to me and said, "Fuck them," a fire in her eyes I hadn't seen in a while. "If anyone doesn't like your story, they're not the people we want anyway." That epitomized Jackie—fierce when circumstances mattered most. Her words settled something in me, a quiet resolve I hadn't realized I'd missed.

That podcast didn't just break my silence. It showed me the power of owning my truth. For the first time since leaving prison, I felt a piece of myself click back into place, like a gear stuck for years finally turning free. I still hadn't grasped how far that truth could reach, though, and how it could ripple out beyond a podcast episode into something bigger. It took stepping into a classroom a few months later to see the real impact, not just on me, but on the kids who needed to hear it most.

THE CULMINATION OF SPEAKING MY TRUTH

A few months after the podcast aired, I got a text from Angel, an AVID teacher at Hamilton High School. She had married a high school buddy of mine, now a Chandler police officer who worked with the FBI. The irony didn't miss me. The same law enforcement world that had once locked me up now invited me to help kids avoid my old path. Angel wanted me to speak to her class about life skills. My visit would be part of a program she ran bringing speakers in to help students navigate their futures. "Your story," she wrote, "could really impact these kids."

Reading her message, I felt excitement mixed with a rush of adrenaline. So far, training athletes and helping people recover defined my comfort zone. Standing in front of a room full of teenagers and formally laying out my past like a blueprint to help guide their future choices represented uncharted territory, but I couldn't wait for this new challenge.

Public speaking tops most people's fears—above death, above spiders, above anything. For me, though, speaking was the fun part. Being vulnerable and exposed with the chance that they'd see me as a cautionary tale gone wrong instead of a comeback worth believing in worried me most. I spent weeks preparing, not just what I'd say, but how I'd say it. I rehearsed my speech every day in my Tahoe on the way to work. I didn't write anything down. I wanted to speak directly from my heart so it would sound authentic. These weren't just any students. They attended Hamilton High, a wealthier school in Chandler, sure, but I knew from experience that money didn't make you immune to bad choices. I'd seen plenty of rich kids in my dealing days, snorting lines off glass tables in gated communities, just as lost as the ones on the Southside.

Walking into that first classroom, I sized up my audience: twenty students with a mix of backgrounds and attitudes. Some sat up front with notebooks open, eager for whatever wisdom I'd drop. Others slouched in the back, arms crossed, eyes half-closed, just killing time until the bell. I could feel them trying to figure me out—this guy in Jordans and a white T-shirt that had the word "Freedom" across the chest, tattoos peeking out from my sleeves, who came to teach them something about life.

I started with a question to catch them off guard. "Any of y'all got some blues I can take real quick to calm my nerves? Maybe a vape pen?" Their shocked expressions turned to nervous laughter, the kind that ripples through a room like a wave. The teacher, Angel, tensed for a second, her clipboard clutched a little tighter, but I saw her relax when the kids leaned in. They knew this wouldn't sound like another boring lecture about saying no to drugs.

For the next hour, I walked them through my journey—from BMX racing as a scrappy kid, to wrestling at Marcos de Niza, to selling drugs in my early twenties because I thought it'd make me somebody, to federal prison where I learned what "somebody" really meant. I told them about the arrest—the cold snap of cuffs on my wrists, the way my mom's voice broke over the phone when I told her I wouldn't be coming home for a while. I told them about the grind of rebuilding—starting over at Rehab Plus, building MOVE with Jackie one client at a time. But more importantly, I talked about conscious choices—how success or failure doesn't depend on one big decision but hundreds of small ones, how every morning you wake up with two paths: one toward who you want to become, the other toward who you want to avoid becoming.

"There's no standing still," I said, my voice steady as I met their eyes. "You're always moving one way or the other."

During the Q and A, a kid in the back raised his hand, his hoodie pulled low over his brow. "How'd you stay positive in prison?" The question caught me off guard, not because it challenged me to answer, but because it showed he thought beyond the surface, picturing himself in a place he didn't want to end up.

"By focusing on what I could control," I replied, leaning against the teacher's desk, my hands gripping the edge. "I couldn't change the walls, the guards, the time. But I could change how I spent my days by reading, planning, and promising myself I'd come out better. I couldn't control what people thought of me, but I could control who I became."

I saw heads nodding, not just his but others'. They might not have served time in prison, but they understood feeling trapped by expectations, by mistakes, by doubts.

Another student, a girl with bright pink nails and a notebook full of doodles, asked, "What's the hardest thing you ever had to tell your family?" I thought about my parents again, that first visit in prison and the worry in my mom's eyes. I remembered my dad's shoulders slumped like the weight of my choices had broken something in him.

"The hardest thing was telling them I'd let them down," I said, my throat tightening. "That I didn't live up to the kid they raised." The room went quiet, the kind of silence that feels like everyone holding their breath at once.

Angel had scheduled me for two classes that day. By the time I finished the second session, my body filled with a fire I hadn't felt before. A student caught me in the hallway afterward. He was a skater kid with a beanie pulled low and his board tucked under his arm. "Thanks," he said quietly, his eyes flicking to the floor then back to me. "I've got some stuff I need to work on, and . . . this helped." I patted him on the shoulder, told him to keep showing up for himself, not anyone else.

Driving home, I called Jackie from the parking lot, the late February sun warm through my windshield. "Remember when we worried about people knowing my story?" I asked her. "I think we got that backward. It might represent the most valuable thing I can offer."

She paused for a moment and laughed softly. "Then you better keep telling it."

Two months later I got a call from Marcos de Niza's athletic director—my old high school, where I'd wrestled in sweat-soaked gyms, where I'd started forming the identity that'd lead me down both good paths and bad ones. They wanted me to speak at an assembly. Walking into that auditorium felt like stepping into a memory I hadn't visited in years. I could almost hear the echo of my teenage self laughing in the halls. I could even almost smell the faint chlorine from the locker rooms where we'd shower after practice. This time, though, I experienced something different. Instead of twenty students in a classroom, I faced more than a hundred, their faces a mosaic of curiosity and skepticism.

Marcos de Niza served a more diverse crowd than Hamilton. These were kids from Tempe, South Phoenix, and Guadalupe. These were the places where I'd grown up, places where temptation lurked on every corner. I spotted them right away: the ones with flannel shirts buttoned to the top, low-key sunglasses perched on their heads, hard expressions that said they'd already seen too much for their age. Those kids represented the ones I needed to reach most.

I opened with the same icebreaker. "Anybody got a vape pen I can hit real quick?" That got the same nervous laughs as the first time I'd asked it. The teachers in the back tensed, exchanging glances, but the students leaned forward, some smirking, some wide-eyed.

"I sat right where you're sitting," I told them, pointing to a row in the middle where I used to doodle in notebooks instead of listening. "Walked the same halls, came from the same neighborhoods. I know some of y'all come from Guadalupe. I used to hang out there too. South Phoenix? Trust me, I know those streets."

I clicked to my first slide—Eddy King's story, the former BMX champion fighting back from paralysis, then Krysten Muir's journey, their own Marcos alumna who'd made history kicking field goals. "These represent just two people I work with at my gym," I said. "But before I could help them overcome their challenges, I had to overcome mine."

I laid it out for them—prison, drugs, hitting bottom, fighting back. I told them about the choice I made in prison to read, to plan, and to redirect the drive that had led me down a destructive path into something positive. More importantly, I hammered home the power of small decisions—how each one either moves you toward your goals or away from them, how the same energy that can destroy you can build you up if you aim it right. The auditorium fell silent, not the restless silence of bored teenagers, but the heavy silence of people recognizing truth. These kids had grown up hearing lectures about making good choices, but here stood someone who'd made the bad ones, paid the price, and found a way back.

When I opened the floor for questions, hands shot up. A kid in a faded hoodie, his voice low but intense, asked, "How'd you go from being a felon to where you are now?"

I thought about all the false starts, the nights I'd doubted myself, the small victories that had built to this moment. "You've got to have a plan," I said, "and stay locked in. My friend Steve Caballero, a legendary skateboarder, told me once: 'Every distraction you let in derails your dream. The more you let in, the further it slips away.' I let distraction derail me once. I refused to let it happen again."

Another student, a girl with braids and a notebook clutched to her chest, asked, "What about prison challenged you most?"

"Losing my freedom," I answered, my voice quieter now. "Not hugging my family, not making my own choices, not living my own life. But the real prison isn't the walls. The cycle of bad choices that got me there created the real prison."

When I finished, the students applauded, but their faces told the story—eyes wide, some glistening, some hard with thought. After the assembly, as I made my way through the hallway, a young Latina girl stopped me, her voice trembling slightly. "Thank you for coming today," she said, clutching her backpack straps like a lifeline. "My brother's in prison right now. He gets out in six months. What advice can I give him about being successful like you when he gets out?" The question hit me hard, a mirror to my own family's hope when I'd been inside. I saw myself in her brother, saw my own sister in her eyes.

"Tell him three things," I said, my voice steady but soft. "Have a plan and stick to it. Don't let distractions get in your way. They'll pull you back faster than anything. And fast money isn't real money. It just gives you a faster way back to prison."

She nodded, scribbling my words on her palm with a pen.

Driving home, the weight of that day settled into me, not heavy like before, but solid and grounding. I thought about that girl's brother, about all the kids in those seats, one choice away from a path they might not walk back from. This work didn't just involve speaking. It represented a mission for me. Every kid who heard my story and chose differently, every family looking for answers, every student who saw a glimpse of possibility in my mess explained why I'd gone through what I had. Hamilton had shown me my story could connect; Marcos showed me it could change lives. And I had only begun to understand what that meant for the road ahead.

THE EIGHTH CODE TO MIND OVER VIRTUALLY EVERYTHING:

Your past mistakes don't define you, but they can refine you.

MOVE Sound Bite Summary

1. When you stop hiding, you stop fighting yourself, and that opens the door to real progress.

2. Painful lessons, when shared honestly, transform into powerful tools to inspire, guide, and heal those who feel alone in their own battles.

3. True transformation doesn't mean erasing who you've been. It means integrating every chapter of your story into who you are now.

4. The road to success leads to your head from your heart. Move toward the person you aspire to become, or drift toward the one you fear becoming. No one stands still; every step counts.

5. Sharing your journey—your flaws, failures, and victories—creates ripples of hope and possibility, reaching people you may never meet but whose paths you can help redirect.

CHAPTER 9

FROM CONVICT TO CEO

"Character, not scholarship, is the foundation of a successful life."
—Calvin Coolidge

As I pulled into MOVE's parking lot, the sun had just begun to rise, casting long shadows across our newly expanded facility. Inside, the morning light filtered through our roll-up doors, catching my reflection in the window. Nothing in my appearance screamed "CEO." No expensive suit and no corner office overlooking a city skyline. Just a guy in Jordan 1 low shoes and a MOVE T-shirt preparing for another day of grinding.

I paused before getting out of my Tahoe and remembered the conversation I'd had with Warren at Rehab Plus years ago. "What are you going to do?" he'd asked when I gave my notice.

"I'm starting my own thing," I'd told him, trying to sound more confident than I felt.

"Shit," he'd replied, "you're going to be fine. Whatever you do, you're going to be great."

I was finally starting to believe him.

For years, I'd thought being a CEO meant looking the part and hiding who I'd been. But now I understood something different. Success doesn't come from sounding like someone else. It comes from being exactly as you are, scars and all.

These moments hit differently now that I'd stopped hiding my past. For years I'd worried that my status as a convicted felon would hurt our business. Instead, embracing my full story had opened doors I never expected. It had also taught me something crucial about leadership—something I'd learned in the streets, refined in prison, and now fully comprehended: Your character drives results much more than your credentials.

This truth had shaped every aspect of how we built MOVE. While other facilities focused on licensure and credentials, we lasered in on impact. This explains why we could succeed as a non-provider-owned physical therapy clinic. It explains why athletes trained alongside recovery patients. And it explains why our team included people like Kaine and Brandon, who started as interns and now led at MOVE.

"You understand that people will train us for free?" That's what the owners of AZ Compass Prep had said when we first connected. But I wasn't worried about working for free. I knew it was an investment. The same mindset guided how we approached physical therapy. Instead of following the traditional model, we created something unique—a place where high-level athletes trained alongside people learning to walk again. Recovery at MOVE also extended beyond the body to include the body and the mind, which meant, to us, the whole person.

This approach raised eyebrows. How could someone without a PT license run a successful therapy practice? The answer was simple, though not obvious: You build a company through character. You find the best people, and you give them room to grow. You create an environment where everyone—staff and clients alike—can become their best selves.

KEVIN JOHNSON

Four weeks before opening MOVE, I got a call from Shaylee Gonzales's father. Shaylee had played basketball at Texas and BYU. She now plays professionally. Her dad told me he had someone named Kevin Johnson who wanted to train with us.

"Kevin Johnson wants to train here?" I said, my mind immediately going to the former Phoenix Suns star point guard turned Sacramento mayor. The name carried weight in the basketball world, and the possibility excited me.

A few weeks later, a man walked through MOVE's doors—six-foot-four with gray hair, dressed impeccably in business casual attire. This man didn't match the Kevin Johnson I'd pictured, but something immediately struck me about his presence. He carried himself with the polished professionalism of someone used to commanding rooms much larger than our 2,700-square-foot facility.

"Welcome to MOVE," I said, extending my hand. "I'm Chad."

That first meeting began what would become one of my most important mentorships. Kevin hadn't played as an NBA star. He had accomplished something arguably more impressive: a self-made success story who'd built CHS Plumbing into one of the largest commercial plumbing companies between Colorado and Arizona. What struck me most wasn't his business knowledge. At sixty-one years old, he came there to train like an athlete, preparing for Team USA basketball competitions in the Masters division.

We started with individual training sessions, but those quickly evolved into something bigger. One day Kevin approached me with an idea. "What if we offered training to all my employees at CHS Plumbing?" he asked. "I'll cover the costs." This opportunity could help MOVE, but it revealed something more important about Kevin's character. He wanted to share what he'd found valuable with his entire team.

Out of roughly fifty local employees, only two showed up. Most business owners would have seen this as a failed experiment and moved on. Instead, Kevin redirected his energy. "What about the kids who need this but can't afford it?" he asked. He started sponsoring local student athletes, particularly those from smaller schools who might otherwise miss out on high-level training. Before long, he supported twenty young athletes at MOVE.

Kevin didn't just write checks. He showed up. After his own 8:00 a.m. daily personal training sessions, he'd return on Saturdays to work out alongside the kids he sponsored. Something remarkable emerged in watching a successful CEO diving on our turf during agility drills, surpassing the intensity of teenagers less than a third his age. He didn't just invest money; he invested himself.

Through Kevin I learned that how you handle success matters more than the success itself. "Always tell the truth, whether it brings good or bad news," he'd say. This represented more than advice. It reflected how he actually operated. During our conversations between sets, he'd share stories with me about his own journey, including the times he'd had to sell his house and rebuild his business from scratch. These didn't signify failures to him. They served as stepping-stones and lessons that shaped his character.

Kevin's approach to business challenged everything I thought I knew about functioning as a CEO. In the construction industry, precision matters. One small miscalculation in plumbing at ground level can result in major problems several stories up.

"We GPS everything," he told me, explaining how CHS Plumbing maintained its reputation for accuracy. "You start right from the very beginning, get the foundation perfect, and everything else follows."

This philosophy extended beyond plumbing into leadership principles. Every detail matters to Kevin; every choice builds on the ones before it. What actually sets Kevin apart, though, isn't just his attention to detail or business sense. It's his understanding that true success doesn't come from dollars and cents, but from impact.

I saw this firsthand in how he treated everyone at MOVE. Whether he trained alongside high school athletes or chatted with other clients, he brought the same authenticity and warmth. He never acted like the successful CEO he embodied. He expressed himself as just Kevin, the guy who'd show up at 5:30 a.m. to work on his basketball game, and then at 8:00 a.m. to train. He also celebrated other people's victories as enthusiastically as his own.

When people ask me about my transition from convict to CEO, they often expect me to tell stories about my business strategies or funding challenges. But my real transformation happened through relationships with people like Kevin. He showed me what character-driven leadership looks like in practice. Success, he taught me, doesn't mean avoiding failure. It means responding to failure, learning from it, and most importantly, using your own failures to help others.

The most important lesson Kevin taught me focused on authenticity in leadership. The business world often pushes people to create polished, perfect images of themselves. Kevin showed me something different. Despite his success—the multimillion-dollar projects, the Team USA competitions, the respect he'd earned throughout the industry—he remained grounded, real, human.

Today, whenever I face a difficult business decision, I often find myself thinking, *What would Kevin do?* The answer usually appears clear: Do what's right, not what's easy. Take care of your people. Use your success to create opportunities for others. These don't just represent business principles. They embody character principles, and they've become foundational to how we operate at MOVE.

A NETWORK OF LEADERS

Kevin's mentorship opened doors to me developing relationships with other successful business leaders. Each of them has shown me different aspects of character-driven leadership. What started with Kevin expanded into a network that would shape my understanding of what it truly means to function as a CEO. These connections didn't form at networking events or chamber of commerce meetings. They grew organically through authentic interactions and shared values.

BRAD CESMAT

Brad Cesmat built Sports360AZ the same way I built MOVE: one relationship at a time, one story at a time. He didn't try to compete with major media outlets by copying their approach. Instead, he carved out his own space by focusing on what he did best: telling authentic stories about local sports. Watching him build his brand taught me that you don't have to follow the traditional playbook to succeed.

As a media veteran, Brad taught me invaluable lessons about controlling your message and understanding your audience. "You speak differently to inmates than you do to CEOs," he told me. This didn't mean being inauthentic. It meant communicating effectively with different groups. Whether he interviewed a twelve-year-old multisport athlete or a Division I quarterback, Brad knew how to adjust his approach while staying true to his core values.

Our paths intersected regularly through the local sports scene. When Tyler Shough went from backup quarterback at Oregon to starting at Texas Tech and Louisville, he needed training, so Brad connected Tyler with us at MOVE. Also, when we had a client's success story to tell about our work with Krysten Muir, for example, Brad helped tell it. He understood intuitively that great stories don't just describe a person's achievements. They chronicle that person's journey and transformation.

Brad's influence on me extended beyond media coverage. He played a crucial role in my development as a public speaker and storyteller. When I started writing this book, he advised, "Keep your phone by you no matter what. When you have any moment, any note that comes to your head, write it down." These practical insights came from Brad's years of experience telling stories that resonated with people.

Through Brad, I learned that building a business involves more than what you do. It's about how you communicate it to the world. You can provide the best service or product, but if you can't tell your story effectively, you limit your impact. The best advice Brad gave me: "Control what you can control."

TIM HOVIK

Tim Hovik, the current chairman of the influential Ford National Dealer Council, came into my life in 2021 through a recommendation by Brad Cesmat when he needed rehabilitation for a hip replacement. As an executive, philanthropist, and owner of San Tan Ford, Tim operates at the highest levels of business leadership. Like many successful people, Tim could have gone anywhere for his recovery. But from the moment he walked through our doors, I saw something different in his approach. He was efficient and focused—the kind of person who'd come in with exactly fifty minutes to spare and maximize every second of it.

Tim taught me something crucial about leadership identity. One day I asked him what made his dealership different from all the others on the corner. His answer cut straight to the point: "Because of me. I make the difference." This wasn't arrogance—it was ownership. In a world where many leaders hide behind corporate speak and careful PR, Tim's directness felt refreshing. He didn't need to pretend to be something he wasn't. His results spoke for themselves.

Tim operates at a level few achieve. He's one of Arizona State University and the Arizona Cardinals' biggest donors. He's also a major sponsor of the Waste Management Phoenix Open. But what strikes me most about Tim is how he treats everyone around him. At his dealership suites during Cardinals games, he rotates different groups through—one week the sales team, the next week the service department. Everyone gets their moment; everyone matters.

When Tim isn't at his dealership, he's constantly in motion—flying across the country and world to pursue new achievements and foster community growth. Tim lives by a "less talk, more action" mentality, focusing on building vibrant communities with robust local economies. His drive for success extends far beyond selling cars; it's about creating meaningful impact everywhere he goes. This 24/7 dedication to networking and supporting communities showed me what true business leadership looks like beyond office walls.

His perspective on business challenged my thinking. When we discussed expanding MOVE, Tim pointed out something crucial. "You can't be everywhere at once," he said. "I don't stay at my dealership all day long. I have employees who run it like a well-oiled machine for me. Yes, I participate in ownership, but you have to build something that can run without you being there every minute."

Tim taught me that real entrepreneurs don't just delegate tasks; they move on to build new projects while their team handles daily operations. His insistence that I needed to get out and network at events reinforced why building a strong team at MOVE was so important. Even when I'm away from the facility, I'm still working—just with a different focus on marketing, networking, and brand development.

When my father first warned me about starting MOVE, he'd said something similar: "You better not just be buying yourself a job." He meant that a real business should operate without the owner doing everything. Hearing Tim reinforce this wisdom years later was a powerful reminder that I needed to transition from a do-everything-all-the-time owner to a true CEO.

Through Tim, I also learned the importance of preserving the human element in business. When many companies moved toward online-only sales, Tim fought to maintain direct sales at his dealership. "It's about the customer's experience," he explained. "The cars are the same, but the experience—that's where we make the difference." This resonated deeply with our approach at MOVE. We didn't just provide services; we created experiences, built relationships, and made a difference in people's lives.

Leaders like Tim, Brad, and Kevin didn't just achieve success—they created significance. That difference between success and significance matters. Success measures what you achieve. Significance measures what you help others achieve. I also noticed none of the leaders I admire spend time talking about their credentials or titles. They focus on creating value, building relationships, and maintaining their character.

Their examples of leadership made me think about my past life in the streets where connections (not relationships) functioned purely as transactions, and trust lasted only as long as it served someone's interests. These CEOs operate differently. They develop relationships with their clients and other people like me. They play the long game. They understand that your reputation—your character—means everything. Just like Kevin's plumbing work, they know that what lies hidden beneath the surface matters as much as what people can see.

BUILDING A BUSINESS THROUGH CHARACTER

Ethics in business isn't an abstract concept. It's about making concrete choices every day that reflect who you are and what you stand for. At MOVE, this translates into specific decisions that shape our culture and impact.

When high school athletes can't afford training but show exceptional drive, we create opportunities rather than turn them away. When a burn patient needs more sessions than insurance will cover, we find ways to make it work. These aren't just nice gestures. They're character decisions that define our business.

The physical therapy landscape has changed dramatically over the decades. In the 1990s, insurance reimbursement averaged around $240 per session, giving therapists ample time to provide personalized care to each patient. Today that same reimbursement has plummeted to around $65 per session in Arizona, forcing many clinics to quadruple their patient loads to maintain financial viability. Meanwhile, large hospital corporations are buying up private practices to leverage higher reimbursement rates that independent clinics can't access.

As a non-provider-owned facility, MOVE faces additional challenges—we receive lower reimbursements than provider-owned clinics. This reality could easily push us toward volume-based care, but we've deliberately chosen a different path. Instead of treating more patients for shorter sessions, we've diversified our business model to include training, rehabilitation, and performance services, allowing us to maintain our commitment to quality care without sacrificing financial sustainability.

As MOVE's CEO, the way I run our small business is different. I can't hide behind layers of management or corporate policies. When something goes wrong, I can't blame the system because my team and I *are* the system. Every day, I work on the floor with our clients, so I see firsthand how our decisions affect people's lives.

That's why I tell our team, "Personality might get people in the door, but character keeps them coming back." The character we've built at MOVE is rooted in our unwavering commitment to our clients' goals and outcomes. We're not a "get them in and out" facility. We're a relationship-based business built on genuine care and proven results.

Our approach to character means showing up consistently for each client, member, and athlete, regardless of their status or profile. When you love what you do, your attitude, personality, and results naturally shine through. We've created a vibrant, supportive atmosphere where success is celebrated with authenticity and good humor. This commitment to character—prioritizing integrity, effort, and attitude over quick profits—is what brings clients back and builds our reputation through word of mouth.

I've always had the personality part down. Even in my darkest days, I could connect with people. But building MOVE required something deeper from me. It required me to develop the kind of character that makes tough choices even when no one's watching, like the time we had to decide whether to expand during COVID. Traditional business strategy said play it safe, wait it out. But we saw people needed us more than ever. We doubled our space, added new programs, took on more complex cases. This represented more than a business decision. It reflected what I call a "character decision."

For example, many businesses would bend over backward to accommodate a "VIP" client. But when a high-profile athlete wants special treatment that would disrupt care for our regular clients, we explain that at MOVE, everyone receives the same high-quality care and attention. Our high-profile athletes respect our integrity and have become some of our strongest advocates.

Jackie and I maintain the same mindset when it comes to the people on our MOVE team. We're not just hiring employees; we're investing in futures. When you've hit bottom, when doors close because of your past, you understand the difference between having a job and having a future.

This future-based mindset has shaped how we develop our team. During COVID, when other facilities canceled internships, we kept ours going. We saw beyond the immediate circumstances to the long-term opportunity. Now Kaine, for instance, has developed into our director of sports performance. This title represents more than a new position and status for Kaine. It creates a career path for him that we're building together.

Brandon came to us through a similar route by starting with us as an A.T. Still University physical therapy intern. Now he directs our physical therapy department, developing innovative treatment protocols and pushing the boundaries of what rehabilitation can make possible for our patients. We're giving Brandon a platform to grow.

For us, creating careers means more than promotions and titles. It means investing in people's growth, even when no immediate payoff exists. I learned this lesson the hard way at Rehab Plus. I felt grateful for that job, especially coming out of prison, but I hit a ceiling. I could only advance so far. That experience taught me something crucial about leadership: If you want to keep good people, you have to show them their future and support them when it's time to let them go live that future.

You're either growing, or you're dying. There's no standing still in business. The same applies to people. If they're not growing, they'll look for growth somewhere else. That's why we invest in our team's education, their certifications, and their development. Yes, that costs money. Yes, sometimes they might take those skills elsewhere. But if you fear losing people, the competition will leave you behind.

BREAKING THROUGH BARRIERS

The journey from incarceration to entrepreneurship revealed not only personal challenges but systemic barriers that affect millions of Americans with criminal records. These barriers don't just hinder individual progress. They limit our entire society's potential.

Most people don't realize how many doors close when you have a felony conviction. It's not just about the social stigma, which is built into the system itself. For example, when I tried to sell medical equipment after prison, I sailed through the initial interviews. My big personality and knowledge got me that far. But as soon as they ran a background check on me, everything changed. It didn't matter that my conviction had nothing to do with medical sales. The door simply closed.

That's why starting MOVE wasn't just about business. It was about survival. When society puts up walls, you have to build your own doors. Statistics show that earning an honest living prevents re-offending better than almost anything else. Yet the system often makes it difficult. If you carry an ounce of the victim mentality post prison, you're not going to make it.

What struck me most working in the prison system was the contradiction at its core. I saw talented inmates developing real skills in prison industries, making products for the same government that would later make it nearly impossible for them to use those skills in the free world. The system teaches you to work, then blocks you from working. It demands rehabilitation, then punishes you even after you've changed.

The same system that locks people up for breaking laws creates exceptions when convenient. This taught me something crucial. You have to focus on what works for you and your team, not what others say you can or cannot do.

This backward system runs deep. Companies can get tax credits for hiring felons, but their insurance policies often prevent them from doing so. Banks encourage small business loans but won't give them to people with records. Society tells former inmates to reform themselves through honest work, then systematically blocks them from most professional paths.

That's why I believe CEOs with criminal records have a special responsibility. We're not just building businesses. We're proving something vital. Your past mistakes don't determine your future success. When people ask how I made the transition from convict to CEO, they're usually looking for some secret formula or special connection. But the truth is simple: You have to outwork the barriers.

When you have a criminal record, society questions your qualifications, and it questions the very core of who you are as a person. This is what I mean when I talk about character in business. While everyone faces scrutiny about their skills or experience, former inmates face a deeper, more fundamental judgment about our integrity, our values, and our moral compass.

In addition to being nice and honest, qualities that matter, character is about consistently prioritizing effort, attitude, and integrity in everything you do. It means focusing on the process over the product, putting who you are before what you achieve. For those of us with criminal records, building and demonstrating character becomes even more crucial because we're constantly working against the stigma of our past convictions.

True character emerges when you consistently choose to do what's right, even when it's difficult or inconvenient. It shows in how you treat people when there's nothing to gain, how you respond to setbacks, and how you handle success. At MOVE, we've built our reputation on getting results and *how* we achieve those results—with integrity, compassion, and an unwavering commitment to our clients' well-being.

Every time I walk into a meeting with potential clients or partners, I know my character has to speak louder than my record. When other CEOs talk about their Ivy League degrees or corporate backgrounds, I talk about results. When they discuss their professional certifications, I show them transformed lives. This doesn't mean I think credentials have no value. It means you can do hard things and achieve excellence in more than one way.

The system may change slowly. Since 2015, for instance, forty states have reduced some licensing barriers for people with criminal records. But change isn't coming fast enough for the thousands of former inmates trying to rebuild their lives right now. That's why businesses like MOVE matter. We're not waiting for the system to change. We're creating new possibilities within it.

Every successful CEO I've met has a different story about overcoming obstacles. But former inmates face a unique challenge. We have to overcome both external barriers and internal doubts. Society doesn't just question our qualifications; it questions our character. Because of that, we have to work ten times harder than the average person to demonstrate the strength of our character.

The solution for those of us who have been incarcerated doesn't involve hiding who we are or pretending our past didn't happen. I tried that approach early on, and it exhausted me. The solution for anyone who has done anything that would have people question their character is to transform your story from a liability into an asset. Your time in the streets teaches you to read people and situations. Prison teaches you patience and resourcefulness. The journey back teaches you resilience. It turns out these aren't just survival skills. They're leadership qualities.

Today when I speak at high schools or business events, I discuss my background directly—not to sensationalize it, but to show what's possible. Every time someone with a record succeeds in legitimate business, it challenges assumptions. Every time a former inmate builds something meaningful, it weakens and reduces the number of obstacles for others.

The true measure of a CEO isn't just their profit margin or market share. It lies in the barriers they break down, the lives they transform, and the futures they help build. That's why I'm sharing my story. Not because it's remarkable, but because it shouldn't be. Thousands of potential leaders sit behind bars who could be building businesses, creating jobs, and transforming lives.

As I look out across our facility each morning, I see more than equipment and square footage. I see the embodiment of a simple truth I've learned over the years: Your character speaks louder than any credential. Your impact matters more than your past. And sometimes the worst chapters of your story become the most powerful tools to help others write better futures for themselves.

THE NINTH CODE TO MIND OVER VIRTUALLY EVERYTHING:

Character drives results—not credentials.

MOVE Sound Bite Summary

1. True leadership comes from who you are, not what you've done or where you've studied.

2. Building through character means making decisions based on impact rather than immediate profit.

3. Every obstacle can become a building block for something greater.

4. Your network should be measured by depth, not breadth. One mentor who genuinely invests in your growth is worth more than a hundred superficial connections.

5. Success means creating pathways where others see dead ends.

CHAPTER 10

FAIL TO PLAN, PLAN TO FAIL

"A goal without a plan is just a wish."
—Antoine de Saint-Exupéry

The first time thirteen-year-old Chantel Osahor walked into Rehab Plus, I knew she was different. Standing more than six feet tall as a freshman, she commanded the room with a presence that made everyone look up. Her knee pain brought her in, but something in her eyes told me she represented more than another injured athlete.

During our first session, as I worked on her knee and started building her recovery plan, she revealed something I almost never hear from high school athletes. "I have a plan," she told me. "I'm going to play college basketball." Most young athletes have dreams, but Chantel spoke about her future with the kind of quiet certainty that made you believe her. And she used the P word: plan.

She possessed talent and practiced discipline, focus, and, most importantly, adaptability. During the next four years, I watched her develop into one of the top basketball players in Arizona. Her St. Mary's High School team accomplished something unprecedented: They became the number-one ranked team in the nation, went 30–0 in the 2011–2012 season, and won the prestigious Nike Tournament of Champions. The core of that team had played together since they were eleven years old. They had a plan, and they executed it to perfection.

But life has a way of testing even the best-laid plans. When Chantel arrived at the University of Washington for her freshman year, her journey took an unexpected turn. On her first day riding her bike to class, a car struck her. The incident left her with a shoulder injury that threatened to derail her entire first season. Some athletes might have seen this as a devastating setback. Chantel saw it as an opportunity to adapt her plan to new circumstances.

During her recovery, she didn't only focus on healing. Instead, she studied basketball from a different perspective, developing an even deeper understanding of basketball strategy and team dynamics. When she finally returned to the court, she brought something extra: a broader vision of the game that would eventually help her set records for rebounds and become one of Washington's most influential players ever.

Here's what separates successful planners from failed ones. Their plans don't function as rigid road maps that shatter on first contact with reality. Their plans serve as living frameworks that bend and adapt while keeping their destination in view. In other words, the plan changes; the purpose doesn't. I've had to learn this lesson repeatedly throughout my life, from my days dealing drugs on the streets to my time in federal prison, from launching MOVE, to expanding it into what it has become today. A plan doesn't just help you reach a destination; it provides a framework that allows you to adapt when circumstances change.

Looking back now, I realize the first meeting with Chantel didn't just revolve around helping a young athlete with knee pain. I witnessed the beginning of someone's journey who understood, even at thirteen, that success requires more than talent or hard work. It requires a plan. More importantly, it requires the wisdom to know when and how to adjust that plan without losing sight of your ultimate goal.

THE POWER OF PLANNING

People dream all day long. They dream about becoming successful, about changing careers, about building something meaningful. But here's what I've learned: A dream without a plan amounts to wishful thinking. The difference between a dream and a goal is simple: Write goals down. The moment you put pen to paper, you begin transforming those abstract hopes into concrete possibilities.

During my years in the drug game, I thought I had a plan. I could get product from South Phoenix, take it up to Scottsdale, and double my money. That seemed like a plan at the time, but it was really just a series of reactions. My immediate circumstances, rather than any larger purpose, dictated each reaction, each move I made. I was drifting without defining my destination, even though I felt like I was in control. I didn't truly understand the difference between having a plan and responding to opportunities until I landed in federal prison.

In prison, I watched two types of inmates serve their time. The first counted days on the wall like notches on a belt—no plan beyond freedom itself. The second type (guys like me) broke down each day into deliberate steps: complete educational courses, make connections, develop skills. We weren't just doing time; we were building a foundation for a successful release. It's not hard to guess which group stays out of prison and which returns. Planning doesn't just help people grow in prison. Creating a plan makes the difference between a person experiencing a permanent transformation or just temporary freedom before getting put back in prison again.

I see this same principle play out every day at MOVE. When new clients come in, I always ask about their goals. Many can tell me what they want—to get stronger, to recover from an injury, to play their sport at the next level. But wanting something isn't enough.

"What's your plan?" I ask them.

The ones who succeed understand the value of a plan. They don't just say they want to get better; they commit to showing up three times a week, following their rehab protocol, and doing their homework exercises.

Here's the crucial part about planning that took me years to understand. Your plan has to mean something to you beyond making money. I don't care if you want to be a pro athlete or run a successful company. If you're chasing money, it's not going to end well. When I dealt drugs, my aim was to make money—and as much of it as possible. That's not a real plan. That's just greed with no strategy. A good plan needs to have a positive purpose, something that drives you beyond the basic pursuit of profit.

I learned this lesson from Kevin Johnson, owner of CHS Plumbing. He didn't just build a successful commercial plumbing company. He built relationships and trust between himself and his customers and between himself and his employees. His plan didn't just cover completing projects. It focused on becoming the best in his field. Kevin cared about doing work so precise and reliable that his reputation spoke for itself. The money followed naturally, but it didn't serve as the primary focus of his business-building plan.

This explains why I tell my clients, especially the young athletes, that their training plan needs to connect to something bigger than just winning games or getting scholarships. What drives you? What deeper purpose motivates you? When you have that clarity, the daily grind becomes meaningful. The early morning workouts, the repetitive exercises, the careful attention to detail—they all serve a larger purpose.

This is the hard truth about plans: You're either working your plan, or you're helping someone else achieve theirs. In prison, I saw this play out every day. The guys who didn't have their own plan inevitably got caught up in someone else's scheme. I watched inmates fall into debt with other prisoners, trading commissary items without a strategy to pay back what they owed. Some would get involved in contraband schemes, assuming they could make quick money, only to find themselves taking the fall when things went wrong. These guys weren't working their own plan; they were disposable pieces in someone else's game.

The same patterns play out in the business world through pyramid schemes and multilevel marketing organizations. These operations succeed by convincing people to set aside their own dreams to serve someone else's profit machine. In sports we're seeing this with the current NIL policies in college athletics, where young athletes get pulled into deals that might benefit them financially in the short term but don't always align with their long-term development as players or people.

Even in everyday life, it's easy to get caught up in society's default plan: working jobs you hate to buy things you don't need to impress people you don't care about. Without your own plan, you become a supporting character in someone else's story.

This is why I'm always preaching to write things down. When you put your plan on paper, it becomes real. You can see it, review it, refine it. You can also share it with others who can help you achieve it. Most importantly, you can hold yourself accountable to it. Dreams live in your head, but the best plans live in the real world where you can act on, measure, and achieve them.

A great plan doesn't just outline a series of steps to reach a goal, though. A great plan builds a framework for making decisions, a filter for opportunities, and a compass for navigating challenges. Without a plan, you wander, hoping to stumble into success. With a plan, you create your own path, even if you have to adjust your route along the way.

CHANTEL'S BASKETBALL JOURNEY

Chantel's basketball journey is a master class in how plans must evolve while staying true to your core purpose. When she arrived at St. Mary's High School, Chantel didn't fit the typical basketball prospect mold. At two-hundred-plus pounds, she didn't match the conventional image of what coaches typically look for. But she possessed something that set her apart: extraordinary court vision and basketball IQ that made her a force on the floor despite her unconventional style.

Chantel's high school career was historic. The team she helped build at St. Mary's dominated. By the time she graduated, Chantel was ranked seventy-first nationally by ESPN. But college basketball presented new challenges. That first-day-on-campus bicycle accident could have ended her career. Instead, it forced Chantel to adapt. When she finally returned to the court, she brought something extra—a perspective that would help her become Washington's all-time leading rebounder.

Chantel's style also defied norms. She didn't jump when she shot. She relied solely on the wrist flick. *Sports Science* on ESPN would later reveal that she had the second-quickest release in basketball, faster than everyone except Steph Curry, the NBA's all-time leading three-point scorer. She even tied the PAC-12 single-season rebounding record with 519 boards in 2016–2017. Then she became the second player in program history to reach a thousand points and a thousand rebounds. Playing alongside future WNBA star Kelsey Plum, Chantel recorded forty-two career double-doubles, the second in program history.

After college Chantel faced another crossroads. She didn't really want to play in the WNBA. Her body had worn down, and she had other aspirations. But she felt a responsibility to the younger girls who looked up to her.

"I don't want to let these girls down," she told me during one of our training sessions as we prepared for the WNBA Draft.

Despite her doubts, she kept training. The Chicago Sky selected her twenty-first overall, then traded her to the Minnesota Lynx. Her WNBA journey was brief. During preseason, after she had two strong games with double-doubles, the swelling in her knee led coaches to suggest she sit out the third game. When she tried to push through, saying she could play, they held her out. The next day, on the plane ride home, the coach approached her. "Hey, number zero, when we get back, you're cut."

Some might have seen this as a failure. Chantel saw it as an opportunity to pivot. She had always displayed intelligence, even skipping eighth grade to play with the older girls in high school. Now, at just twenty-four years old, she had an opportunity to become a coach. But true to her methodical nature, she didn't rush into a head coaching position when the opportunity arose.

"If I fail as a head coach now," she told me, "I'll never get another chance. I need to learn, to build my résumé, to do this right." This wasn't defeat—it was strategic planning. She took a graduate assistant position at Drake University, then joined her former Washington coach Mike Neighbors's staff at Arkansas. They made it to the NCAA Tournament, and the program achieved its highest ranking since 1995.

Today Chantel works at Gonzaga as an assistant coach, continuing to evolve her coaching style while maintaining her core principles. In a recent text message, she shared how one of her players told her, "I haven't felt a presence like yours since being at Gonzaga. Thank you for being that person and having my back." This meant everything to Chantel because it showed she achieved her true purpose—not just coaching basketball but also impacting young athletes' lives.

Her journey exemplifies the difference between having a plan and dreaming. Her core purpose never centered only on basketball. She focused on excellence, on making an impact, and on showing other players what's possible when you refuse to limit yourself with conventional thinking. Every time Chantel's path shifted, she adapted her plan while staying true to that deeper purpose.

WHEN PLANS GO WRONG

My most expensive business lesson cost me two years in federal prison because drug dealers are great at perfecting their entry strategy but neglect their exit plan. We can calculate supply routes, profit margins, and customer acquisition with military precision, but ask any dealer "What's your five-year exit strategy?" and watch their expression go blank. The same blindness kills legitimate businesses every day. Founders obsess over launch strategies but rarely plan for who and how someone else will take over for them: "succession planning." Athletes train relentlessly for competition without planning for career transitions. The pattern is universal. Without an exit strategy, your success becomes your trap.

When I was dealing, I had a solid plan for sourcing drugs in South Phoenix and selling them in Scottsdale. I knew how to make deals, build connections, and maximize profits. I performed my entry strategy flawlessly, but I never planned for how my illegal "business" dealing drugs would end. When you're young, cocky, making money, and everything seems to be going well, you don't think about your exit. You convince yourself you're too smart to get caught, too careful to make mistakes.

This is why I spend so much time talking with our young athletes about life beyond sports. "What's your plan if you get injured?" I ask them. "What's your backup strategy?" Most of them look at me like I'm trying to rain on their parade. Having a backup plan doesn't mean you lack confidence. It means you're a strategic thinker who's prepared for all possibilities.

When you don't control your plan, your plan ends up controlling you. I witnessed this firsthand during my time dealing drugs. What started as a business venture to make extra money gradually took over my life. The money flowed well, but soon I started using the product myself. The plan I thought I controlled now controlled me. This pattern can repeat itself in legal businesses, too, when entrepreneurs become slaves to their companies, athletes become prisoners of their success, or coaches lose sight of their original purpose.

Even with a plan, businesses can fail, but failure doesn't have to mark the end of a particular path you think you're on. Every failed plan carries lessons if you're willing to learn them. When I got out of prison, I could have seen my criminal record as the end of my professional aspirations. Instead, I studied what went wrong. I hadn't just failed because I got caught. I'd failed because my plan lacked purpose beyond making money. My new plan with MOVE had to be different. It couldn't just be about money; it had to be about impact.

Sometimes, though, people fail to plan simply because they're afraid—afraid of commitment, afraid of failure, afraid of success. I see this in the gym all the time. People come in wanting to transform their bodies or recover from injuries, but they resist making concrete plans. They'd rather keep their goals vague so they won't feel too disappointed if they don't achieve them.

Others fail to plan because they focus too much on immediate gratification. In prison I saw guys who could plan elaborate schemes to get contraband but couldn't plan their first month out of prison. They mastered short-term strategy but remained completely blind to long-term possibilities or consequences. This same limited mindset got most of us in there in the first place—focusing on immediate gains while ignoring ultimate costs.

One key way to think about planning gone wrong is learning to see setbacks as setups for comebacks. When Crystal, our first physical therapist at MOVE, decided to leave and focus on virtual therapy, it could have derailed our whole operation. Instead, we used that moment to reevaluate our structure. Then we brought in Brandon as our director of physical therapy, and our program became even stronger. In the long run, the "failure" of our original plan ultimately led to a better plan.

Looking back at my own journey, every major success came after a significant setback. Getting arrested forced me to reevaluate my life's direction. Losing our house to keep MOVE alive taught us what we were truly made of. The COVID-19 pandemic, which could have destroyed our business, ended up transforming it into something stronger than we'd imagined.

The hard reality is plans fail, but that's not the problem. The problem stems from not having a plan at all—or not learning from the failures when they happen. Every time a plan falls apart, you have two choices: You can let the failure defeat you, or you can use it as feedback to modify your plan. Failure is data for your next attempt.

BUILDING BETTER PLANS

Building an effective plan is like constructing a house. You need a solid foundation, strong supporting structures, and enough flexibility to withstand whatever storms may come. Through my years of working with athletes, patients, and running MOVE, I've learned that the best plans share certain key components.

First, every plan needs a clear purpose. The plan doesn't just outline what you want to achieve. It explains why you want to achieve it. When I work with athletes recovering from injuries, we don't just plan to get them back on the field. We plan to make them stronger, more resilient, and better prepared than they were before the injury. The "why" drives the "how."

Second, plans need to operate on multiple timelines. Coach Art Dye's "one in a row" philosophy doesn't merely involve taking one small step after the other; it involves planning those steps deliberately. Each step, each "one in a row" doesn't occur randomly. Choose your steps strategically to build toward your ultimate goal. At MOVE, every single rep we assign, every single exercise we program serves as a planned stepping-stone or one deliberately placed brick in a larger structure we're building together.

I tell my athletes constantly, "The separation is in the preparation." Your preparation determines your separation from the competition. You can't just show up on game day and expect to perform. This principle also applies beyond sports. When we prepared to open MOVE, for example, I spent months planning every detail, from equipment layout to marketing strategies. That preparation gave us an edge when we finally opened our doors.

But preparation doesn't mean rigidity. One of the biggest lessons I've learned is plans need built-in flexibility. When COVID hit, many gyms and rehabilitation centers had to shut down because their plans couldn't adapt to the new reality. We survived and thrived because we'd built our operation with enough flexibility to pivot when circumstances changed.

Here's my planning framework for how I structure a game-changing plan. I've given you some space to begin answering the questions below that will help guide your thinking as you structure your own game-changing plan.

A GAME-CHANGING PLAN IN NINE STEPS

Step 1: My Core Purpose: What am I truly trying to achieve?

_____

Step 2: Success Metrics: How will I measure progress?

_____

Step 3: Daily Actions: What specific steps will I take every day?

_____

Step 4: Weekly Milestones: What should I accomplish each week?

_____

Step 5: Monthly Goals: What bigger achievements am I targeting?

_____

Step 6: Potential Obstacles: What might get in my way?

_____

Step 7: Contingency Plans: How will I adapt if things go wrong?

_____

Step 8: Support Team: Who will help me stay accountable?

_____

Step 9: Evaluation Schedule: When and how often will I review and adjust my plan?

_____

The key to creating a game-changing plan is understanding the difference between your core purpose and the specific methods you use to achieve it. Any method (a process, technique, or strategy you'll use) might need to change as you execute your plan, but your purpose should remain constant.

When I worked with Eddy King on his spinal cord injury recovery, for example, our purpose to regain his mobility and independence never changed, but we constantly adjusted our rehabilitation methods based on what worked and what didn't at any given moment. For instance, one of the last times I was stretching Eddy, his hip popped out due to his paralysis and Legg-Calvé-Perthes disease. We knew it was time for a total hip replacement. It's very rare for a paraplegic person to have this operation, but we knew we needed it done to continue our plan of care so he could walk again.

As you're planning, you'll need to keep short and long-term planning in mind. Short-term planning deals with immediate action steps, like what needs to happen today, this week, this month. Long-term planning covers direction and development, like where you want to be in a year, five years, ten years. The art is in connecting these timelines, so your short-term actions build toward your long-term goals.

You also need regular evaluation points. At MOVE, our communication flows daily rather than waiting for formal meetings. Jackie continually updates our team on insurance and billing matters as they evolve. I work directly with our trainers and therapists every day, discussing new methodologies and addressing challenges in real time. This continuous feedback loop means we're constantly refining our approach based on what's working.

Building in contingencies is crucial. I learned this the hard way in my previous life before prison because having only one plan, one way forward, leaves you vulnerable when things go wrong.

Now I always have backup strategies. If a treatment approach doesn't work for a patient, I have alternatives ready. If a business initiative doesn't deliver results, I have other options to explore.

In business, results come from effective marketing and branding. When a social media campaign isn't performing as expected, we can pivot to in-person community events. When digital advertising isn't reaching our target audience, we leverage our existing client relationships for testimonials and word-of-mouth referrals. For instance, after helping Tim Hovik with his rehabilitation, he offered to mention MOVE on his radio advertisements as a thank-you. This kind of authentic endorsement often delivers better results than traditional paid advertising. Service remains key to our results, but strategic marketing drives our growth.

The most important element in building game-changing plans involves understanding that they function as living documents. They should grow and evolve as you do. When we first opened MOVE, our plan focused on survival—make enough to keep the doors open. As we grew, our plans also grew to include expansion, new services, community impact. Each phase built on the previous one while adapting to new opportunities and challenges.

The ultimate test of a game-changing plan isn't whether it works exactly as you envisioned. It hinges on whether the plan keeps you moving forward, even when circumstances change. Think of it like a GPS system: When you take a wrong turn, a GPS doesn't give up and shut down. It recalculates, finding a new route to the same destination. Your plans should work the same way.

WHAT'S NEXT

Standing in MOVE today, looking at our "Wall of Character" covered with jerseys and mementos from lives we've helped transform, I see how far we've come and how far we still have to go.

When Jackie and I first opened our doors, the plan was just to survive one week at a time. Now, as we approach our tenth year, our vision has expanded far beyond those initial dreams of survival.

As you probably guessed, we've mapped our ten-year plan in detail with timeline markers and contingency pathways. By 2030 we'll break ground on a 15,000-square-foot comprehensive performance center with integrated medical facilities, recovery pool, and adaptive training zones. These aren't just dreams and wishes. We're already meeting with architects, researching financing options, and identifying potential locations. Each quarterly business review brings us one step closer to this vision.

Jackie and I see this future facility as more than a business asset. It represents an investment in our legacy. When we prepare to retire, this property will embody our life's work and a continuing resource for our community. We aim to build something that will outlast us, something that can continue making a difference long after we've stepped away.

My plan for myself extends beyond the physical expansion of MOVE. Through my speaking engagements at places like Hamilton High School and Marcos de Niza, I've discovered a new way to make an impact. When I share my story with teenagers, I tell them about my past, but I also show them what's possible for their futures. Every time a parent tells me their kid saw things differently after hearing me speak, I realize this offers another way to fulfill our mission of transforming lives.

Publishing this book represents another step in that evolution because I'm offering you a blueprint for how you might face your own struggles. I've written each chapter, each lesson learned, to offer you tools to build your own path forward. The ten codes I've shared with you throughout this book don't just represent my philosophy for living a fulfilling life. I mean for them to be practical guides for you to navigate your own life's challenges.

At this point in my own journey, I'm evolving from being a business owner who must focus on daily operations to becoming a true CEO who focuses on the vision and impact of our business and beyond. This shift from business owner to CEO means Jackie and I are developing our team so they can handle more of the day-to-day operations while I focus on expanding our reach and influence.

My business mentors Kevin Johnson, Tim Hovik, and Brad Cesmat have shown me what this evolution to become a CEO looks like and how to execute on that vision. It involves creating systems that allow your business to thrive, even when you don't directly involve yourself in every decision. It means building a team that shares your vision and values. This also means people like Brandon and Kaine receive the training and development to become future leaders in their own right—maybe even CEOs, if they want.

Part of MOVE's evolution and my own evolution involves giving back to the community in bigger ways. I remember sitting in that courtroom years ago expressing remorse, not just for my crimes but for all the families my actions had affected. Now I have an opportunity to help others avoid the same paths to make amends. I want to show them how they can create better ways forward.

Every time I work with a young athlete, every time I help someone recover from an injury, every time I share my story with students, I fulfill the promise I made to myself in prison—to make my second chance count.

None of this happens now or in the future without maintaining what made MOVE successful in the first place—our commitment to transforming lives through movement and mindset. As we grow, as we expand our influence, this core purpose remains unchanged. Whether we work with professional athletes, rehabilitation patients, or students in a classroom, our mission stays the same: helping people move better, think better, and become better.

The journey from convict to CEO hasn't come easy, but it's taught me that with the right plan, the right purpose, and the right people, anything is possible. As we move forward with these plans for growth and expansion, I remain focused on the lesson that has brought us this far: Success isn't just about what you achieve; it's about who you help along the way.

THE TENTH CODE TO MIND OVER VIRTUALLY EVERYTHING:

Failing to plan is planning to fail.

MOVE Sound Bite Summary

1. Dreams become goals when written down. Dreams exist in your mind; plans exist in the real world.

2. Purpose powers planning. Without meaning, a plan amounts to just a strategy for accumulation.

3. Plan your exit, not just your entry. How you finish matters more than how you start.

4. Build flexible plans with fixed purposes. Let your path bend without breaking your direction.

5. Preparation determines separation. Your readiness today creates your advantage tomorrow.

CONCLUSION: A GAME-CHANGING PLAN FOR YOUR FUTURE

Before you close this book, grab a pen. Right now, write down *one* specific action you'll take in the next twenty-four hours. Not something vague like "eat better" or "work harder." Write something specific and measurable like "prepare three healthy meals tomorrow," or "wake up at 5:30 a.m. to write for thirty minutes."

Writing one specific, measurable action down isn't just about your intention; it's about your commitment. One concrete action written down and committing yourself on paper is the first step to starting your own transformation.

No paper around? No problem. Write it down directly in this book. Here's some space:

_____

_____

_____

Nice work! Positive change begins with the smallest movements.

You've just completed a journey through ten fundamental codes for transforming your life, but this isn't really about codes or systems—or even about my story. It's about you and your potential for transformation.

Perhaps you picked up this book because you face your own struggles. Maybe you're trying to rebuild your life after setbacks, launch a business, recover from injury, or simply become a better version of yourself. Whatever brought you here, know this: You have everything you need to change your life. The power to change doesn't reside in these pages; it lives inside you.

Throughout this book you've learned that your identity doesn't remain fixed, that your choices shape your future, that your environment influences your outcomes, and that optimism doesn't just signify an attitude—it offers a strategic advantage. You've seen how character drives results, how pain can lead to growth, and how having a plan is essential for success.

But knowledge isn't enough. These lessons only matter if you put them into action. Start with one small change—one conscious choice, one environmental adjustment, one step in your plan. Remember: Transformation happens one step at a time, one choice at a time, one day at a time. One in a row.

You may think, "But my circumstances differ," or "You don't know what I'm dealing with." You're right—everyone's journey is unique. But the principles of transformation apply universally. Whether you're in a prison cell or a corner office, recovering from injury or building a business, the same fundamental truths apply: You become who you choose to be, your environment shapes your possibilities, and your mindset determines your outcomes.

Your past mistakes or current circumstances don't define you. Your next move, your next choice, your next step forward is what matters most. Your transformation journey begins now. Not tomorrow, not when conditions are perfect, not when you feel more ready—now. Take these codes, these lessons, these principles, and make them your own. Adapt them to your situation. Use them as tools to build your future.

The path ahead won't always be easy. You'll face setbacks, doubts, and obstacles. But remember this: On the other side of pain lies greatness. Beyond every challenge awaits an opportunity for growth. Through every struggle comes a chance to become stronger.

This isn't just about moving better physically. It's about moving better through life. It's about thinking better, choosing better, becoming better. It's about creating a life of purpose and impact, regardless of where you're starting from.

Remember the core message that's guided us through these pages: Mind Over Virtually Everything (MOVE!). When you truly internalize this principle, you recognize only two forces can truly stop you: a lack of faith in yourself and natural disasters. Everything else? Those are temporary obstacles your mind can overcome.

The choice now belongs to you. The tools rest in your hands. Your future's waiting to be written. What will your story be?

Move forward. Move with purpose. Move toward the life you want to create. Move with belief in your potential. Live with passion! Let's go! Let's go, baby!

ACKNOWLEDGMENTS

To my wife, Jackie. Thank you for loving me through every version of myself, for challenging me, and for always believing in the man I could become. You've loved me at my lowest and still stand beside me as we rise. Your strength, honesty, and relentless support have shaped not only this book, but the man I've become. Thank you for being my partner, my inspiration, and the heart behind everything I do. You've helped me become him.

To the community, all our clients, patients, and athletes. You're the people who have stood by me, encouraged me, and reminded me of my purpose every step of the way. Your support gave me the courage to keep MOVING forward, even when the path was not clear. Whether you knew it or not, your words, presence, and energy helped shape the foundation for this process. As I've said from the beginning, "MOVE, it's for the people."

To my MOVE family. Thank you for always helping me grow, for believing in the vision, and for building something meaningful to me. Kaine and Jamie, your assistance and daily listening mean the most. Brandon, I appreciate your attention and thoughts as I brought topics to you day after day. Berlin, thank you for jumping in with genuine interest and becoming part of the MOVE story so quickly. Koby, welcome to a true team. You'll now see the "why" behind it all.

To my parents, in-laws, sister, and all my family. Thank you for believing in me with consistency, patience, and unconditional love. You've always seen my potential, but we know what they say about potential. You all saw it and encouraged me all the way; your strength has built my foundation. Chastin and Ava, thank you for your support and conversations that helped shape this journey. Collin and Mak, I appreciate your feedback and input more than you know. And to my daughter Jade, I hope you're reading. This one's also for you.

To the staff at Peacock Proud Press. Thank you for your time, patience, and guidance. A special thank you to Laura Bush, CEO, and Kristin Watson Heintz, project manager, for directing me through the publishing process with care and clarity. Your belief in this book helped bring it to life.

And finally, thank you to James Thole. Your role in this project was far more than just ghostwriting. You helped me find words when I couldn't, gave structure to the chaos, and turned personal stories into powerful messages. This book wouldn't be what it is without your voice behind mine. I'm deeply grateful we wrote this and cheered through the different sports seasons together.

Much love to all,
Chad Dunn

ABOUT THE AUTHOR

Chad Dunn is the co-founder and CEO of MOVE Human Performance Center and Physical Therapy in Chandler, Arizona, where he combines physical training and mindset coaching to help people transform their lives. His journey from nationally ranked BMX racer to convicted felon to successful business owner has given him a unique perspective on human potential.

After serving two years in federal prison, Chad rebuilt his life by focusing on what he does best—helping others move beyond their limitations. Whether working with professional athletes, people recovering from catastrophic injuries, or youth seeking direction, he brings the same message: On the other side of pain lies greatness.

A certified behavioral change specialist with over twenty years of experience in the health, modern fitness, and sports performance fields, Chad has helped everyone from NFL and NBA players to people recovering from catastrophic injuries. His greatest joy comes from helping ordinary people achieve extraordinary results, from helping individuals with spinal cord injuries walk again to helping severe burn victims regain movement and independence.

Today, Chad splits his time between running MOVE, speaking to audiences about personal growth, and working directly with clients. He lives in Mesa, Arizona with his wife and business partner Jackie, who helped him build MOVE from the ground up.

Want to connect with Chad or hire him as a speaker?
Email info@moveperformance.com

www.ingramcontent.com/pod-product-compliance
Lightning Source LLC
Chambersburg PA
CBHW031317120626
46554CB00001BA/441